KUBERNETES

A Simple Guide to Master Kubernetes for Beginners and Advanced Users

(2020 Edition)

Brian Docker

The content within this book has been derived from various sources. Please consult a licensed professional before attempting any techniques outlined in this book.

By reading this document, the reader agrees that under no circumstances is the author responsible for any losses, direct or indirect, that are incurred as a result of the use of the information contained within this document, including, but not limited to, errors, omissions, or inaccuracies.

TABLE OF CONTENTS

Introduction

At the core of containers are features called control groups (or cgroups). Cgroups are important because they allow the host to limit and also share resources that each container utilizes. This is important for several reasons, including proper allocation of resources to ensure that each container functions smoothly

It also impacts security and prevents certain attacks, such as denial-of-service attacks. A distributed denial-of-service attack, or DDoS, is a cyberattack in which the attacker removes access to a certain machine or software.

This way, the real owner of those components might find out that the work he or she has been performing becomes unavailable to him or her. This allows the attacker to carry out changes, install malicious software, and cause other forms of harm. In some cases, they can indefinitely disrupt the services of the host.

But those are not the only benefits that containers are able to provide. Containers allow for easy application creation and their deployment. Containers can increase efficiency and make work faster for the developer.

Containers are also able to provide constant development, integration, and deployment features. This allows developers to receive reliable and frequent build and deployment. They are also able to perform their tasks with quick and easy rollbacks.

When developers are using containers, they have a certain consistency across platforms. They can run, test, and produce their applications the same way on the laptop or other computing device as they do in the cloud. This is because they have access to the containers no matter where they access them from.

Resources are isolated and this allows for users to predict the performance of the application. When they are able to predict performance, they can make corrections whenever necessary and are able to get an overall idea of what the end result might turn out to be.

There is more efficiency in the way the resources are utilized as well. Typically, working outside of containers might lead to wasting resources, but containers ensure that applications work with a specific number of resources.

While recognizing some of the features of containers, it is also important to grasp the concept of namespace. Namespace is an important feature in Kubernetes that allots resources to various containers. It also connects various processes together.

This allows different processes to interact with each other efficiently. Namespaces also place a limit on the level of visibility that one process has on other ID components, filesystems, and networking. A container process then becomes restricted. This allows for each container to work independently without any outside influence or effects, which could affect the integrity and quality of the process.

Furthermore, users can also utilize union file systems. To understand what a union is, we have to look at the game Tetris. This might take you by surprise, but there is a reason for using this example. What union does is take the files and directories of different file systems and creates one single file system comprising of the individual file systems.

Think of each file system as one part of a Tetris block. Each block is of a different shape, but if you get them together, they form straight rows. However, if you break apart the rows, you can still get the individual parts. This is the same with union. You can still utilize each of the individual components, but they are all stacked together to form a single file system.

This is convenient because having different file systems means that work becomes more complicated and it is longer to perform a task.

So the big question is, why should you use Docker?

Containers on their own are not a new technology and have actually been around for many years. There are many applications that can run it. However, what truly sets Docker apart from other applications is the ease of use it has brought to the community. Docker promotes the use of Continuous Deployment and Continuous Integration.

This means that even when you have to troubleshoot something or there are certain updates you have to run, there is no delay in progress. These methods, when utilized properly, can have a great impact on your software product's results and quality.

Chapter 1. How Kubernetes Operates

Kubernetes ' element is that the audience. A cluster consists of machines or virtual, which each serves a role as a node or as a master. Each node hosts collections of a couple of containers (which comprise your software), and also, the master communicates with nodes around when to make or ruin containers. It educates nodes to re-route traffic according to fresh container alignments.

The Kubernetes master

The Kubernetes master is your access point (or the controller airplane) by which administrators and other users to interact together with the bunch to deal with the scheduling and installation of containers. A bunch will have a minimum of one master but might have more based on the replication pattern of the cluster.

The master stores the configuration and nation information for your bunch in ectd, a continuous and information that is dispersed store. Every node has access, and via it, nodes know how to keep the configurations.

It is possible to operate, etc. Experts communicate with the rest of the audience the entry point into the management airplane, tube-apiserver.

By way of instance, the kube-API server makes certain ·that configurations from the, etc. Match configurations of containers set up from the bunch. Control loops are handled that by the kube-controller-manager handle the audience via the Kubernetes API server's condition. Replicas deployments and nodes have controls.

By way of instance, the control is responsible for tracking its health and registering a node. The tracks and handled workloads from the bunch kube-scheduler. This service assigns a function to nodes and keeps track of the resources and capacity of both nodes. The cloud-controller-manager is a service Kubernetes which can help maintain it "cloud-agnostic."

Nods

All nodes at a Kubernetes cluster should be configured using a container runtime, which can be Docker. The container runtime handles and begins the containers since Kubernetes set up to nodes from the cluster them. Your softwares (web servers, databases, API servers, etc.) Run within the containers. Every Kubernetes node conducts a broker procedure called a sublet.

That is accountable for keeping application containers based on directions from the management plane: starting, stopping, and handling the condition of this node.

The sublet gathers performance and wellness data from pods, the node, and containers it conducts and shares that data with the management plane to help scheduling decisions are made by it. The Kube-proxy is a cluster. Also, it functions as a load balancer for solutions.

The scheduling unit is a boxer container that may share resources and ensured to be co-located on the server system. Each pod has been assigned a unique IP address inside the bunch, allowing the program to use vents. You describe the condition of these containers at a pod via a JSON or YAML thing known as a pod spec. These items are passed into the sublet via the API server.

Pod

A pod can specify a couple of volumes, like a disc that is local or system expose them into the containers at the pod, which permits containers, and disk.

Volumes may be utilized when a single container downloads material, along with also another container upload those articles.

Since containers pods are ephemeral, and Kubernetes provides a sort of load balancer, referred to as a service, to simplify sending orders. A service aims a logical pair of pods chosen according to labels (explained below). You can enable access to them, although, by default, providers could be accessed from inside the bunch.

Deployments and replicas

Setup is a thing that defines the pods and the variety for every pod, known as tractors, of container cases. You specify the number of replicas you would like to have running in the audience. By way of instance, if a node expires, the copy set will guarantee that a different pod is scheduled on another node.

A daemonset deploys and runs on the particular daemon (at a pod) on nodes you define. They utilized to supply pods with maintenance or services. There is, by way of instance, a place new relic infrastructure receives the representative.

Namespaces

Namespaces permit you to make clusters physical bunch. Namespaces are meant for use in environments that have many users spread over projects or teams. They isolate bunch tools and assign source quotas.

Stateful sets and steady storage volumes

You are given the capability by stateful sets keep networking between components, pods in the event you want to move pods into nodes, or persist data between them. Likewise, storage tools are provided by persistent storage volumes to get a bunch to which pods can request access since they're deployed.

Additional Helpful elements

These Kubernetes elements are helpful but not mandatory for normal functionality.

Kubernetes DNS

Kubernetes provides this mechanism for support discovery involving pods. This DNS server functions also.

Cluster-level logs

It is possible to incorporate it with if you've got a tool Kubernetes save and to extract network and program logs from inside a bunch, composed to standard error and standard output. It is essential to be aware that Kubernetes doesn't offer log shipping if you would like to utilize logs; you must provide your log storage alternative.

The way that it can make your job easier and stress-free as an individual

- Kubernetes helps you maneuver Quicker. Kubernetes permits you to produce a self-explanatory Platform-as-a-Service (PaaS), which produces a hardware layer abstraction for development teams. Your development teams can economically and easily request. Since assets come in infrastructure, if they want more funds to handle the load, then they could find those as fast. You are filling out forms to Ask your application to run. The only provision and proceed get the most out of this tooling developed around Kubernetes for automating packaging, installation, and testing, for example, Helm (more below).

- Kubernetes is cloud-agnostic. Workloads can move without needing to redesign your software or fully rethink your infrastructure, which enables you to prevent vendor lock-in and standardize on a stage.

- Suppliers that are cloud will handle Kubernetes for you. Kubernetes is clear, as mentioned earlier, Normal for container orchestration tools. It must come as no surprise; then, those cloud suppliers are currently providing lots of Kubernetes -as--Service- offerings. Google Cloud Kubernetes Engine, amazon EKS, Azure Kubernetes Service (AKS), Red Hat Openshift, and IBM Cloud Kubernetes a Kubernetes platform control is all provided by service, so you can focus on what matters to you.

Chapter 2. Kubernetes Deployment

Kubernetes Deployment, as per the official documentation, involves the user "describing the desired state in a Deployment object, through which the Deployment controller changes the actual state to the desired one at a controlled rate."

Prior to examining how Deployments specifically operate, it is important to consider that Kubernetes is an object store that also has code that is specifically designed to interact with the objects. Moreover, every object that is stored has 3 components: specification, current status, and metadata. The user's role is to provide the metadata, along with a specification where the desired state of each object is thereby described. Kubernetes works to ensure that this desired state manifests.

With regard to deployments, Kubernetes deployments oversee services that are stateless and can run on your cluster, rather than StatefulSets, which tend to manage stateful services. The purpose of deployments is to ensure that sets of identical pods are kept running and are then upgraded in a manner that is controlled. This is to say that rolling updates are performed by default.

You should also note that "Replicas" in key names refers to the specific number of pods that are replicated, as opposed to the number of ReplicaSets. Also, consider the following with regard to Kubernetes deployments:

- Replicas are copied directly from the spec. In a brief interval, you can read a deployment specifically where spec.replicas are not congruent with status.replicas.

- availableReplicas refers to the number of pods that are readily prepared for some time (minReadySeconds). As a result, this will certainly assist with preventing flapping of state.

- unavailableReplicas refers to the overall number of pods that you should ensure are present, minus the number of pods that have yet to be produced.

- updatedReplicas are the overall number of pods that are reachable by this specific form of deployment, as long as they match the spec template.

- readyReplicas are the total pod numbers that can be reached from deployment all the way through each of the replicas.

Kubernetes employs Conditions in many different areas of its platform. These are all lists of condition objects. Keep in mind that the very minimal object will contain a status, type, and reason.

Once you are equipped with a Kubernetes cluster, you are then able to deploy all of the containerized applications along with it fully. In order to do this, you will have to formulate a configuration of Kubernetes Deployment. In addition, the Deployment will inform Kubernetes on how to produce and update different instances of the system.

After you have finally produced a Deployment, the Kubernetes master will schedule each mentioned applications and systems onto Nodes within the cluster.

Thereafter, when these application and system instances are produced, a Kubernetes Deployment Controller will begin to monitor each of those instances. Moreover, if the Node hosting a particular instance is deleted, the Deployment controller will then replace it. This is important because it will provide a mechanism of self-healing that effectively addresses machine failure as well as maintenance.

Prior to pre-orchestration, scripts for installation tended to be used primarily for starting certain applications. However, they would not allow for effective recovery from machine failure.

Through simultaneously and independently producing application instances and maintaining their operation along Nodes, Deployments with Kubernetes offers a very different approach to management of applications.

Interestingly, you are able to manage and even create a Deployment quite easily by utilizing the Kubernetes command line, which is referred to as Kubectl. Further, Kubectl makes use of the Kubernetes API to engage with clusters.

When you begin to produce a Deployment, you will be required to be specific with the container image that you choose to incorporate for your application as well as the overall number of replicas that you wish to run. Also, you can adjust this information afterword simply by updating Deployment.

Remember that Kubernetes will automate deployment, application scaling, and operations. However, the goal of Kubernetes does not only pertain to system management, but it is also designed to assist all developers as well.

In other words, Kubernetes should ease the process through which distributed services and applications running within datacenter and cloud environments are written.

In order to trigger this, Kubernetes makes two primary designations: Kubernetes will define an API for applications that are containerized to engage with the particular management platforms, along with defining a certain API for administrators so that they can perform particular actions for effective management.

While much of the work on defining an API for applications that are containerized to interact with management platforms are still in the process of being refined, there have been some key features that have stemmed from this process already:

- The Kubernetes mechanism of Graceful Termination offers containers an increased amount of time before it is terminated, this may be due to a maintenance node drain, or even an update that is occurring on a rolling basis, and or a multitude of other reasons. This will allow an application to be shut down more efficiently without any hindrances.

- ConfigMap lets applications read configuration directly from Kubernetes as opposed to employing flags that are command-line.

- Readiness probes ensure a configurable application HTTP endpoint, although other forms are also supported. This allows for determining whether the container in question is ready to be the recipient of traffic and whether it is even alive.

Moreover, this specific function and response will determine if Kubernetes will restart the container and or decide to incorporate it within the pool of load balancing for its service.

Deployments stand for a distinct collection of identical and multiple Pods devoid of any unique identities. It is important to note that a Deployment operates many different replicas of certain applications. This also replaces, in an automatic manner, replaces all particular occurrences when using the platform or else it will not respond. As a result, Deployments make sure that at least one, but likely more, of the instances that you encounter with your application are made available to serve all requests from the user.

Now, Deployments employ a template for Pods. This contains a certain specification for Pods. Moreover, the Pod distinction will ultimately determine the manner in which every Pod appears.

This includes certain applications that are to operate within containers, along with which volumes the Pods are to mount. Once a Deployment's Pod template is altered or morphed in some particular way, brand new Pods will be produced in an automatic fashion, one at a time.

Now, deployments are perfectly tailored for applications that are stateless and that employ only ReadOnlyMany features and volumes that are tethered to various replicas but are far from being a good fit for workloads that utilize ReadWriteOnce volumes. On the other hand, for stateful applications utilizing ReadWriteOnce features, StatefulSets is the best feature to use.

These sets are designed to unload clustered and stateful applications that preserve information and data to storage that is persistent. Compute Engine is an example of this.

Producing deployments can be achieved by utilizing a few different commands. To name just a few, these include: Kubectl create, Kubectl run, and Kubectl apply. One these are produced, the Deployment will make sure that the user's desired amount of Pods will operate effectively, without glitches, and are available everywhere.

Moreover, Deployment will immediately replace all Pods that reach failure or are removed from nodes.

Updating deployments can be achieved by making certain alterations to Deployment's Pod template feature. Enforcing certain changes to this feature field will immediately cause a rollout of an update.

In a default manner, whenever a Deployment is triggered and whenever an update ensues, the Deployment will halt the Pods and then diminish the overall amount of Pods to zero. Thereafter, it will terminate and drain the Pods altogether. The Deployment will then utilize the updated Pod template to raise brand new Pods.

Old Pods will not be taken out of the system until there are a sufficient amount of newer Pods that are up and operating. New Pods will not be produced until enough of the older Pods have been taken out. If you wish to view which Pods, and in what order, are brought forth and then removed from the system, users can run certain functions that the platform will provide.

Deployments make sure that, at the very least, one less than the total number of desired replicas is operating. In this instance, only one Pod, at the most, will be unavailable.

Finally, the life cycle and status of Deployments is worth deeper consideration. Notably, Deployments will be found in one of 3 different states at any particular time: Failed, Completed or Progressing.

A Failed state demonstrates that the Deployment has found one or more problems inhibiting it from finishing tasks that it has been assigned.

Granted, some of these causes will include permissions and or quotas that are not sufficient, along with runtime errors, limit ranges or image pull errors. A

Next, a Completed state suggests that Deployment has effectively finished all tasks that it has been assigned. In addition, this state indicates that all of the Pods are operating with the latest variation and are currently available. Also, this state suggests that there are no old Pods that are up and running.

Lastly, a progressing state suggests that the Deployment is currently in the process of performing particular tasks, such as scaling Pods and or bringing them up to the fore. If users wish to investigate further about the specific causes of a Deployment's failure, they can examine all of the messages within the field labeled status:conditions.

Chapter 3. Kubernetes Pods

A pod (as a pod of whales or pea pods) is a team of one or more containers (such as a docker container), with a shared storage/neck, and a specification for how to run the containers. The content of the pod is always co-located and co-scheduled and operates in a shared context.

A pod model is an application-specific "logical host" - it consists of one or more utility containers that are very tightly coupled - in a pre-container world, being completed on a single physical or virtual computing device Which will be done on the same logic. The host.

The pods allow you to keep connected containers close to the network and hardware infrastructure. Data can live near the application, so processing can be done without generating long delays due to network travel. Similarly, shared data can be stored in volumes split between multiple containers.

The pods basically allow for the logical grouping of containers and parts of our applications.

Now, let's create a directory for our definitions. In this example, we will create a folder in the subfolders / sample books of our home directory:

$ mkdir book examples

$ cd book examples

$ mkdir 02_example

$ cd 02_example

You will see a lot of information, such as floor status, IP address, and even relevant log events. You will notice that the floor IP address is a private IP address. We cannot access directly from a local computer. Don't worry, because the kubectl exec command reflects the functionality of Docker execution.

labels

Tags are simple key-value pairs. You will see them in subsystems, replication controllers, replica kits, services and more. The label serves as the selector and tells Kubernetes resources to collaborate on various operations. Think of it as a filtering option.

We will explore labels in more detail in this chapter, but first we will explore the three remaining constructs: services, replication controllers, and replica sets.

The container's afterlife

As Werner Vogels, CTO of AWS, famously said everything fails all the time; containers and cases can and will crash, become ruined, or maybe even simply get accidentally shut off by a cumbersome admin jabbing around on one of the nodes. Solid strategy and security practices like implementing least benefit curtail a portion of these episodes, yet involuntary workload slaughter happens and is essentially a fact of operations.

Fortunately, Kubernetes gives two truly valuable develops to keep this grave affair all cleaned up behind the curtains. Services and replication controllers/replica sets enable us to keep our applications running with little interference and graceful recuperation.

Services

Services allow us to abstract access away from the buyers of our applications. Utilizing a reliable endpoint, clients and other programs can access cases running on your cluster seamlessly.

K8s achieves this by making sure that each hub in the cluster runs an intermediary named kube-intermediary. As the name proposes, the activity of kube-intermediary is to intermediary communication from a service endpoint back to the comparing unit that is running the actual application.

Participation of the service load balancing pool is controlled by the utilization of selectors and labels. Units with matching labels are added to the list of candidates where the service forwards traffic. A virtual IP address and port are utilized as the section focuses for the service, and the traffic is then forwarded to a random unit on a target port characterized by either K8s or your definition document.

Updates to service definitions are observed and coordinated from the K8s cluster master and propagated to the kube-intermediary daemons running on each hub.

Right now, kube-intermediary is running on the hub have itself. There are plans to containerize this and the kubelet as a matter of course later on.

Replication controllers and replica sets

As you start to operationalize your containers and cases, you'll need a way to turn out updates, scale the quantity of duplicates running (both here and there), or basically guarantee that at least one instance of your stack is always running.

RCs create a significant level mechanism to make sure that things are operating effectively across the whole application and cluster.

RCs are just charged with guaranteeing that you have the ideal scale for your application. You characterize the quantity of unit replicas you want running and give it a template for how to create new cases. Much the same as services, we will utilize selectors and labels to characterize a case's participation in a replication controller.

Kubernetes doesn't require the exacting behavior of the replication controller, which is ideal for long-running procedures. In fact, work controllers can be utilized for brief workloads which allow occupations to be rushed to a fulfillment state and are appropriate for batch work.

Replica sets, are another sort, as of now in Beta, that speak to an improved variant of replication controllers. Right now, the main distinction comprises of having the option to utilize the new set-based label selectors as we will find in the accompanying examples.

Our first Kubernetes application

Before we proceed onward, we should take a glance at these three ideas in real life. Kubernetes ships with various examples installed, however we will create another example from scratch to illustrate a portion of the ideas.

We already created a case definition record, however as you learned, there are many advantages to running our cases via replication controllers.

This is the main resource definition document for our cluster, so how about we take a more intensive look. You'll take note of that it has four first-level components (kind, apiVersion, metadata, and spec). These are regular among all top-level Kubernetes resource definitions:

Kind: This discloses to K8s the sort of resource we are creating. In this case, the sort is

ReplicationController. The kubectl content uses a solitary create command

for all kinds of resources. The advantage here is that you can easily create various resources of various kinds without the requirement for determining individual parameters for each sort. In any case, it necessitates that the definition documents can recognize what it is they are determining.

apiVersion: This essentially reveals to Kubernetes which rendition of the schema we are utilizing.

Metadata: This is the place we will give the resource a name and also indicate labels that will be utilized to search and choose resources for a given operation. The metadata component also allows you to create annotations, which are for the non-recognizing information that may be helpful for customer apparatuses and libraries.

Finally, we have spec, which will vary based on the sort or kind of resource we are creating. In this case, it's ReplicationController, which guarantees the ideal number of units are running. The replicas component characterizes the ideal number of units, the selector component advises the controller which cases to watch, and finally, the template component characterizes a template to launch another case.

The template segment contains the same pieces we saw in our case definition earlier. An important thing to note is that the selector values need to match the labels values indicated in the unit template. Recollect that this matching is utilized to choose the units being managed.

Presently, how about we take a gander at the service definition:

apiVersion: vl

kind: Service

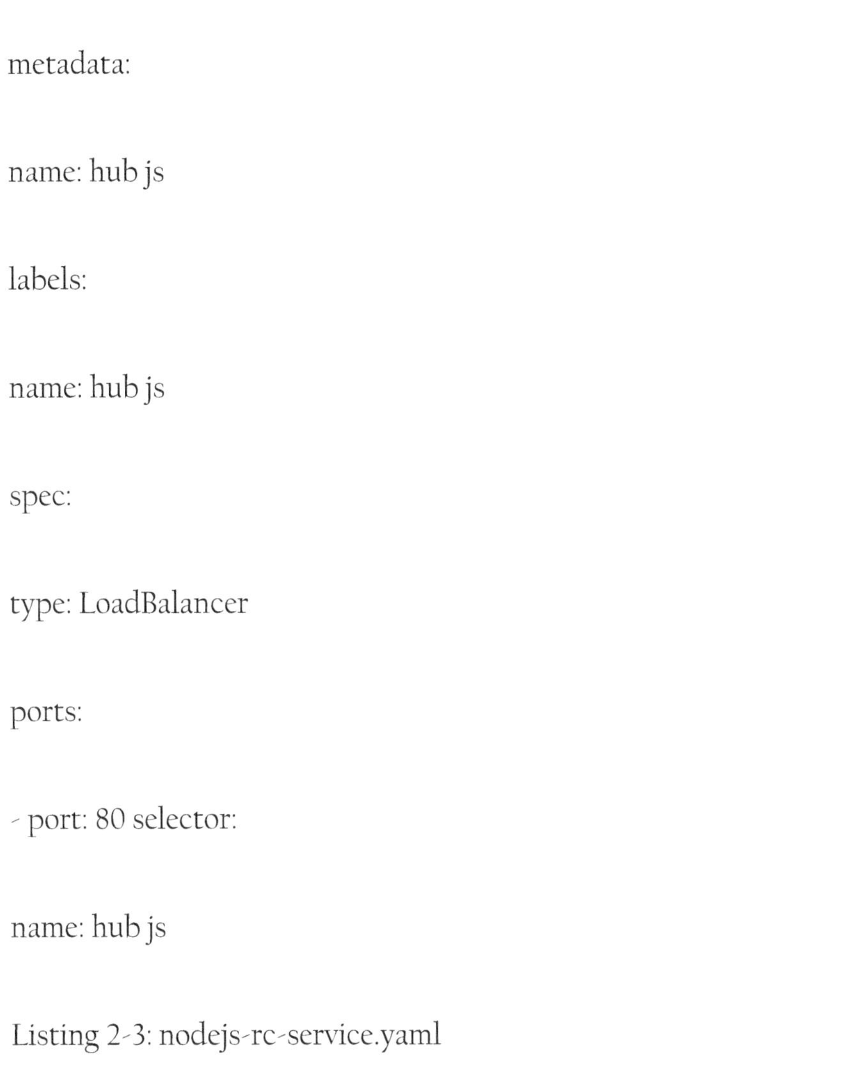

metadata:

name: hub js

labels:

name: hub js

spec:

type: LoadBalancer

ports:

- port: 80 selector:

name: hub js

Listing 2-3: nodejs-rc-service.yaml

The YAML here is similar to ReplicationController. The main contrast is found in the service spec component. Here, we characterize the Service type, listening port, and selector, which tell the Service intermediary which units can answer the service.

Kubernetes bolsters both YAML and JSON formats for definition documents.

On GCE, this will create an external load balancer and forwarding rules, however you may need to add additional firewall rules. In my case, the firewall was already open for port 80. Be that as it may, you may need to open this port, especially in the event that you convey a service with ports other than 80 and 443.

Alright, presently we have a running service, which means that we can access the Node.js servers from a reliable URL. We should take a glance at our running services:

$ kubectl get services

In the first image (Services listing), we should take note of that the hub js service is

running, and in the IP(S) segment, we ought to have both a private and an open

(130.211.186.84 in the screen capture) IP address. In the event that you don't see the external IP, you may

need to wait a moment for the IP to be allocated from GCE. How about we check whether we can associate by opening up people in general address in a program:

You should see something like the figure Container data application . In the event that we visit on numerous occasions, you should take note of that the container name changes. Essentially, the service load balancer is rotating between available units on the backend.

Programs usually cache pages, so to really observe the container name change, you may need to clear your cache or utilize an intermediary like this one:

https://hide.me/en/intermediary

How about we take a stab at playing chaos monkey a piece and murder off a couple of containers to perceive what Kubernetes does. So as to do this, we have to see where the cases are actually running. To start with, how about we list our cases:

$ kubectl get cases

Presently, how about we get some more details on one of the cases running a hub js container. You can do this with the depict command with one of the case names listed in the last command:

$ kubectl depict unit/hub js-sjc03

You should see the first yield. The information we need is the Node: area. How about we utilize the hub name to SSH (short for Secure Shell) into the (follower) hub running this workload:

$gcloud process - venture "‹Your venture ID›" ssh - zone "‹your gce zone›" "‹Node from

case describe›"

Once SSHed into the hub, on the off chance that we run a sudo docker ps command, we should see at least two containers: one running the pause image and one running the actual hub express-data image. You may see more if the K8s booked more than one replica on this hub.

Except if you are really fast you'll probably take note of that there is as yet a hub express-data container running, yet look carefully and you'll take note of that the container id is extraordinary and the creation time stamp shows just a couple of moments ago. On the off chance that you return to the service URL, it is working as normal. Feel free to leave the SSH session until further notice.

Here, we are already observing Kubernetes playing the job of on-call operations guaranteeing that our application is always running.

We should check whether we can discover any proof of the outage. Go to the Events page in the Kubernetes UI. You can discover it by navigating to the Nodes page on the main K8s dashboard. Select a hub from the list (the same one that we SSHed into) and look down to Events on the hub details page.

You should see three late occasions. Initially, Kubernetes pulls the image. Second, it creates another container with the pulled image. Finally, it starts that container again. You'll take note of that, from the time stamps, this all happens in under a second. Time taken may vary based on the cluster measure and image pulls, yet the recuperation is exceptionally brisk.

You may notice that if you open your browser in the direction of the load balancer, the load balancer always responds with the page. You can find the IP address of the load management tool using the kubectl get services command.

This happens for several reasons. First, the status check fails not only because / status does not exist, but the page on which the service shows still works normally between restarts. Second, livenessProbe is only responsible for restarting the tank during a state control failure. There is a separate preparation probe that will remove the container from the endpoint group in the answer service under.

Let's change the status control of a page that exists in our container to get proper status control. We will also add an availability check and refer it to a nonexistent status page. Open the nodejs-health-controller.yaml file and edit the specifications section

Match List 2-8 and save it as nodejs-health-controller-2.yaml:

apiVersion: vl

Type: ReplicationController

metadata:

name: node-js

tags:

name: node-js

Specifications:

Replicas: 3

selector:

name: node-js

Model:

metadata:

tags:

name: node-js

Specifications:

tanks:

- name: node-js

image: jonbaier / node-express-info: last

connectors:

- containerPort: 80 living spaces:

HTTP httpGet status check:

way: /

Port: 80 InitialDelaySeconds: 30 timeoutSeconds: 1

readinessProbe:

HTTP httpGet status check:

route: / country /

Port: 80 InitialDelaySeconds: 30 timeoutSeconds: 1

Example 2-8: nodejs-health-controller-2.yaml

This time, we will remove the old RC that kills the pods and create a new RC with our updated YAML file:

$ kubectl remove rc -l name = node-js

$ kubectl create -f nodejs-health-controller-2.yaml

Now, when we describe one of the pods, we only see the creation of pods and tanks. However, you will notice that the IP load balancer no longer works. If we execute the command described in one of the new nodes, we see an error message about the availability check, but the subkey continues to run. If we change the path of the free / busy probe: /, we can respond again to the main requests for service. Open nodejs-health-controller-2.yaml in the editor and make this update immediately. Then delete and recreate the replication driver:

$ kubectl remove rc -l name = node-js

```
$ kubectl create -f nodejs-health-controller-2.yaml
```

Now the IP load balancer should work again. Hold these modules as we will reuse them. Networks, load balancers and Ingress.

Chapter 4. Kubernetes Services

A kubernetes service is generally considered a REST object. Indeed, this is very similar to a kubernetes pod. In the same way as all of the REST objects, a SERVICE is signified by having the ability to get included in your apiserver in order to produce an entirely new instance. Say, you have a set of PODs and that all of them expose your port 9376 then possess an "app=MyApp" label.

This particular specification is able to produce a brand new Service object that is labeled as "my-service" that will then target TCP port 9376 on any specific Pod that carries the label of "app=MyApp."

Interestingly, the targetPort can refer to the same of a port in the backend Pods. In this way, the targetPort can be a string. The specific number that is thereafter assigned to that name does not have to be the same in each of the backend Pods.

Consequently, this will provide more deployment flexibility and will allow for Services to evolve. To exemplify, you are able to alter the number of the pros that each pod exposes in the subsequent version of your software backend. This can be done without having to break clients.

Take note that kubernetes Services are capable of supporting protocols for TCP, SCTP, and UDP. The default setting is TCP.

Services commonly abstract kubernetes Pods' access; however, they are also capable of abstracting other backend forms. For instance, you should aim to have a database cluster (external) during production; however, when testing, you should use databases that are your own. Also, you should strive to aim your service to a different service that can be found within another Namespace, or even within another cluster altogether.

It is important to note that because you're transferring all of the existing workloads to kubernetes, several backends will then operate externally to it. Now, considering this, you are able to define a certain service without also including a selector.

Proxy-Mode

With regard to this mode, kube-proxy keeps watch over the Kubernetes master for the specific elimination of Endpoints as well as Service objects. This then enables access to a port that is selected randomly on your local node for each specific Service.

Note that any particular connections related to this port are to be proxied to one of the backend Pods of the Service—just as it is reported in Endpoints. Any backend Pod that is used will be determined in accordance with your SessionAffinity for each Service.

Finally, this will automatically install iptables rules designed to encapsulate all of the traffic to the Service's virtual cluster along with the Port and will redirect all of the traffic to the proxy port responsible for proxying the backend Pod. Notably, the selection of the backend is round-robin (this is done by default).

There are particular environmental variables for Kubernetes Services that should be considered as well. For example, whenever a Pod is operated on a Node, the kubelet will then add a stack of environment variables for every active Service in the system. Moreover, it will then support both of the Docker links.

Thankfully, this process will not require any order. Instead, any Service that a specific Pod is trying to acquire access to will have to be produced prior to the Pod itself. If not, the variables within the environment will be unpopulated. However, this restriction does not apply to DNS systems.

With regard to DNS systems, it is strongly recommended (though optional) add-on for a cluster is a DNS server. The DNS server will survey the Kubernetes API for all new Services and will then create a stack of DNS records for all of them as well. If, for instance, DNS is made accessible within your entire cluster, every single Pod will then have the capability of performing name resolution of all Services. on their own.

Headless Services

On certain occasions, however, you will not be required to incorporate load-balancing and single service IPs. For the said instance, it is necessary to produce "headless" services by providing the destination "None" to your cluster IP.

The said option then facilitates all developers in limiting Kubernetes systems coupling by allowing more autonomy to perform discoverer on their own.

Applications will still be able to use a pattern of self-registration. Also, all other forms of discovery systems can be built rather easily on this specific API.

As such, for the said Services, a cluster IP will not be allocated as kube-proxy and will not handle any of these services for you—and the platform will not conduct proxying and load balancing.

The specific way in which DNS is configured will entirely hinge on if the service contains selectors that are defined.

For defined selectors, endpoints controller will create Endpoints records within the API. Also, they will modify the DNS configuration so that it returns A records pointing to Pods backing the Service.

Devoid of selectors, Endpoints controller will not produce records for Endpoints. Nonetheless, the DNS system will configure and search for the following:

CNAME records for ExternalName-type services.

Publishing Services

Now, for certain aspects of the application that you are using, front ends are an example, you might wish to reveal a particular Service directly on an IP address that is external (located on the outside of a cluster).

Kubernetes ServiceTypes will enable greater specification of the exact type of service that you wish to retrieve. Remember that your preliminary setting is ClusterIP.

Type values, along with these values' specific behaviors, are the following:

ClusterIP: It reveals the service directly on an IP that is cluster-internal. This is significant because selecting this value will allow the service only to be accessible from inside of the cluster. Notably, ServiceType is the default.

NodePort: It reveals each Node's IP service at a port that is static. Also, a ClusterIP service that the NodePort service is designed to route to will be produced automatically. This will allow you to more easily contact the NodePort service externally from the cluster through the following request: <NodeIP>:<NodePort>.

LoadBalancer: It is responsible for exposing service in an external manner by employing a load balancer from a cloud provider. In this way, ClusterIP and NodePort are produced (the external load balancer will route to this).

ExternalName: It maps the specific service to each of the contents within the field of the externalName. It does this by returning, with its value, a CNAME record. Remember that no proxy is going to be set up in this scenario. A version of 1.7 or above of kube-dns will be needed.

The Kubernetes master is then going to automatically assign a port from a field determined through your ServiceNode; this is only in instances where you first establish the type field to NodePort. Thereafter, all of the Nodes will then proxy the port into the service that you are using- with the same port number on all of the Nodes. The port will be reported directly into your Services field.

If you wish to select certain IPs so that you can proxy your port, your nodeport-addresses kube-proxy flag should be set to specific blocks of IP. This has been supported since v1.10 Kubernetes.

To retrieve a particular port number, you are able to select a certain value in a nodePort field. Then, your chosen port is then going to be assigned to you by the system. If this path is not chosen, the API transaction will not succeed. Also, keep in mind that you are required to care for any collisions with the port on your own. Not to mention, the specific value that you select will have to be within a configured range for node ports.

Thankfully, it affords programmers their autonomy of establishing their respective load balancers and create environments not supported by Kubernetes in their entirety.

On providers of Cloud, which are responsible for supporting load balancers that are external, establishing the Type field to LoadBalancer will provide for your Service its own load balancer.

Producing the land balancer occurs in an unsynchronized manner, and all of the information therein pertaining to the balancer will be directly punished within the field. Moreover, all of the external load balances' traffic is then going to be directed to your backend Pods. The exact process in which this will operate will entirely depend upon whatever cloud provider is being used. Note that a considerable number of cloud providers do permit for loadBalancerIP to be given a specification.

For these instances, the load-balancer will be produced with the chosen loadBalancerIP. In case, however, that your loadBalancerIP isn't given a specification, another IP will be assigned to this loadBalancer (this new IP will be ephemeral). On the other hand, if the loadBalancerIP is given a certain specification, but the feature is unsupported by the cloud provider, the field will not be acknowledged.

For internal load balancing, it may be vital to direct all traffic from services existing within the same VPC that is being used. Note that this is primarily needed within a mixed environment. In contrast, within a DNS environment that is split-horizon, you will be required to utilize 2 specific services in order to route internal and external traffic toward your endpoints.

Chapter 5. Kubernetes Design Patterns

Before we wrap up this underlying hands-on part, we should take a gander at another method for investigating your Kubernetes cluster.

Up to now, you've just been utilizing the kubectl command-line apparatus. If you're more into graphical web user interfaces, you'll be happy to hear that Kubernetes additionally comes with a friendly (yet at the same time advancing) web dashboard.

The dashboard enables you to list every one of the Pods, Replication Controllers, Services, and different articles conveyed in your cluster, just as to make, modify, and erase them.

Although you won't utilize the dashboard in this book, you can open it up whenever to rapidly observe a graphical perspective on what's sent in your cluster after you make or modify protests through kubectl.

Getting To the Dashboard When Running Kubernetes In Gke

If you're utilizing Google Kubernetes Engine, you can discover the URL of the dashboard through the kubectl cluster-information command, which we previously presented: $ kubectl cluster-

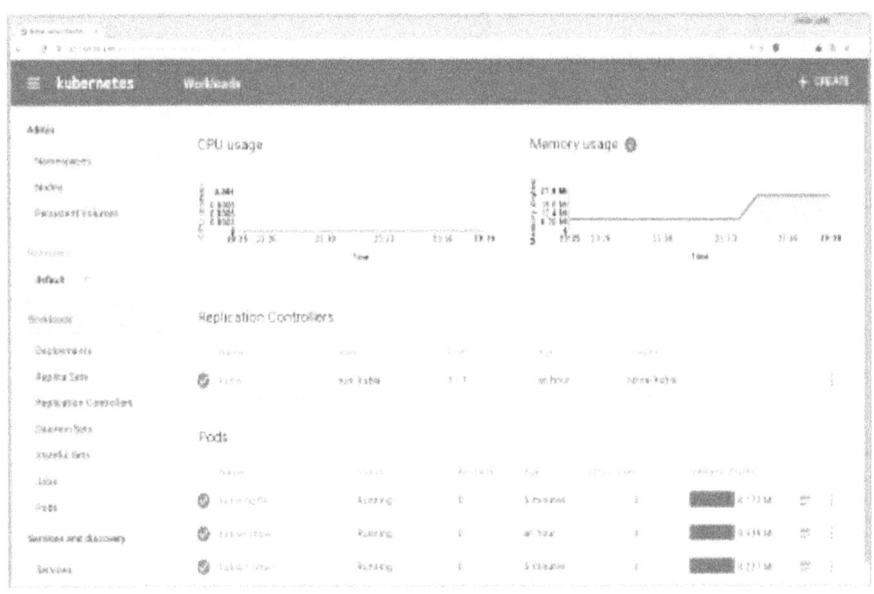

Fig 3.1. Kubernete Dashboard

If you open this URL in a program, you're given a username and secret word brief. You'll discover the username and secret word by running the accompanying command: $ gcloud container clusters portray kubiagrep-E "(username password):" secret phrase: 32nENgreEJ632A12, username: administrator

Getting To the Dashboard When Using Minikube

To open the dashboard in your program when utilizing Minikube to run your Kubernetes cluster, run the accompanying command: $ minikube dashboard.

The dashboard will open in your default program. Not at all like with GKE, won't you have to enter any certifications to get to it.

Summary

Ideally, this underlying hands-on part has given you that Kubernetes is certifiably not a confusing stage to utilize, and you're prepared to learn inside and out pretty much every one of the things it can give. Subsequent to perusing this section, you should now know how to

 Pull and run any openly accessible container picture

 Package your applications into container pictures and make them accessible to anybody by pushing the images to a remote picture vault Enter a running container and investigate its environment

 Set up a multi-hub Kubernetes cluster on Google Kubernetes Engine

 Configure a moniker and tab fruition for the kubectl command-line instrument

 List and review Nodes, Pods, Services, and Replication Controllers in a Kubernetes cluster

 Run a container in Kubernetes and make it available from outside the cluster

 Have an essential feeling of how Pods, Replication Controllers, and Services identify with each other

 Scale an application on a level plane by changing the Replication Controller's imitation tally

 Access the electronic Kubernetes dashboard on both Minikube and GKE

Kubernetes – Core Ideas and Constructs

Kubernetes' general design Prologue to center Kubernetes builds, for example, pods, services, replication controllers, and labels understand how labels can ease management of a Kubernetes cluster Understand how to screen services and container health Understand how to set up planning limitations dependent on the accessible cluster Resources

The design

Although Docker brings a supportive layer of deliberation and tooling around container management, Kubernetes carries comparable help to organizing containers at scale just as overseeing full application stacks.

K8s climbs the stack giving us development to manage management at the application or service level. This gives us computerization and tooling to guarantee high accessibility, application stack, and service-wide versatility. K8s likewise permits better control of resource use, for example, CPU, memory, and plate space over our structure.

Kubernetes gives this more significant level of organization management by giving us key builds to join various containers, endpoints, and data into full application stacks and services. K8s then provides the tooling with to deal with them at the point when, where, and what number of the stack and its components.

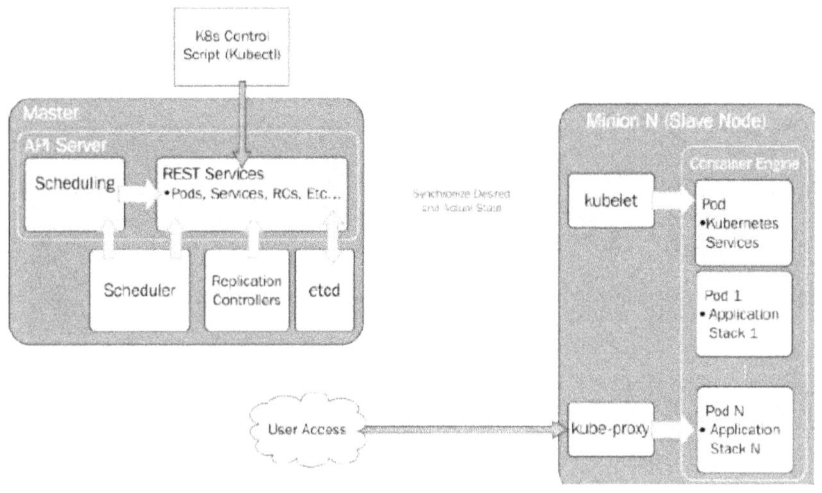

Figure 3. 2. Kubernetes center design

We see the center engineering for Kubernetes.

Most authentic connections are made using the kubectl content or Restful service calls to the API.

Note the thoughts of the ideal state and real state cautiously. This is vital to how Kubernetes deals with the cluster and its workloads. Every one of the bits of K8s is continually working on screening the current real state and synchronizing it with the ideal state characterized by the overseers using the API server or kubectl content. There will be times when these states don't coordinate; however, the system is continually working to accommodate the two.

Understanding the design of a Kubernetes cluster

We've seen a bird's-eye perspective on Kubernetes' engineering. Presently how about we investigate What a Kubernetes cluster is made out of. At the hardware level, a Kubernetes cluster is made out of numerous nodes, which can be part into two kinds:

 The master hub, which has the Kubernetes Control Plane that controls and oversees the entire Kubernetes system

 Worker nodes that run the genuine applications you convey

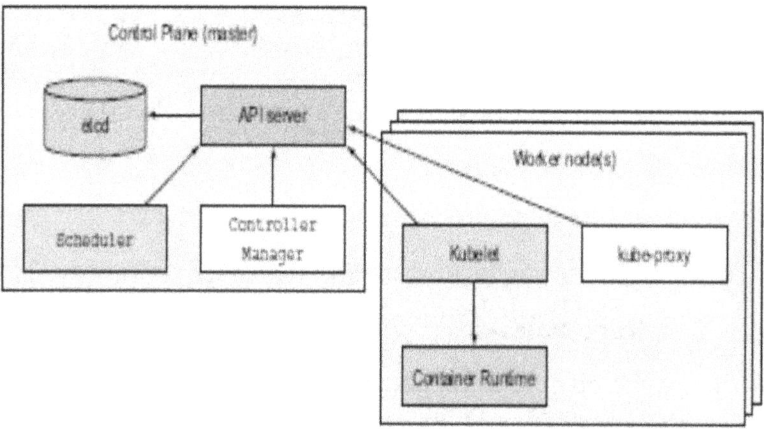

Fig 3.3

The components that constitute the Kubernetes cluster

The Control Plane

The Control Plane is the thing that controls the cluster and makes it work. It comprises of different components that can run on a single master hub or be part over numerous nodes and duplicated to guarantee high accessibility. These components are

 The Kubernetes API Server, which you and the different Control Plane components speak with

 The Scheduler, which plans your applications (allots a worker hub to each deployable component of your application)

 The Controller Manager, which performs cluster-level capacities, for example, repeating components, monitoring worker nodes, handling hub disappointments, and so on

Etcd, a dependable conveyed data store that always stores the cluster configuration.

The components of the Control Plane b maintain and check the condition of the cluster; however, they don't run your applications. The (operator) nodes finish this.

The Nodes

The worker nodes are the devices that run your containerized applications.

I'm not a fanatic of clarifying how things work before first defining what something does and instructing individuals to use it. It resembles figuring out how to drive a vehicle. You would prefer not to realize what's in the engine.

You first need to figure out how to drive it from guide A toward point B. simply after you learn step by step instructions to do that do you become inspired by how a vehicle makes that conceivable. All things considered, comprehending what's in the engine may some time or another assist you with getting the vehicle going again after it stalls and leaves you stranded along the edge of the street.

Running an application in Kubernetes to run an application in Kubernetes, you first need to package it up into at least one container pictures, push those pictures to a picture vault, and then post a depiction of your application to the Kubernetes API server.

The portrayal incorporates data, for example, the container picture or pictures that contain your application components, how those components are identified with each other, and which ones should be run co-found (together on a similar hub) and which don't.

For every component, you can likewise specify what number of duplicates (or copies) you need to run. Moreover, the depiction also incorporates which of those components give service to either inside or outer customers and ought to be uncovered through a single IP address and made discoverable to different components.

Understanding How The Description Results In A Running Container

While the application is running, you can choose you to need to increment or decline the number of duplicates, and Kubernetes will turn up extra ones or stop the overabundance ones, individually. You can even leave the activity of choosing the ideal number of duplicates to Kubernetes. It can consequently continue altering the number, because of continuous measurements, for example, CPU load, memory utilization, questions every second, or some other metric your application uncovered.

Hitting a moving target

We've said that Kubernetes may need to move your containers around the cluster.

This can happen when the hub they were running on has fizzled or because they were expelled from a center to prepare for different containers.

If the container is giving a service to outer customers or different containers running in the cluster, how might they use the container appropriately if it's always moving around the cluster? And in what manner can customers associate with containers giving a service when those containers are duplicated and spread over the entire cluster?

To enable customers to discover containers that give a specific service adequately, you can tell Kubernetes which containers give a similar service, and Kubernetes will uncover all of them at a single static IP address and open that address to all applications running in the cluster.

This is done through environmental factors; however, customers can likewise look into the service IP through old fashioned DNS. The kube-intermediary will ensure associations to the service are load adjusted over every one of the containers that give the service.

The IP address of the service remains steady, so customers can generally interface with its containers, in any situation, when they're moved around the cluster.

Master

The master is the cerebrum of our cluster.

Here, we have the center API server, which keeps up Restful web services for questioning and characterizing our ideal cluster and workload state.

It's imperative to note that the control sheet as it were gets to the master to start changes and not the nodes straightforwardly.

Furthermore, the master incorporates the scheduler, which works with the API server to plan workloads as pods on the real crony nodes.

These pods incorporate the different containers that make up our application stacks. Of course, the fundamental Kubernetes scheduler spreads pods over the cluster and utilizes different nodes for coordinating case imitations. Kubernetes likewise permits specifying essential resources for every container so that these extra factors can adjust booking.

The replication controller works with the API server to guarantee that the right number of case copies are running at some random time. This is a model of the wanted state idea. If our replication controller is characterizing three copies and our real state is two duplicates of the case running, at that point, the scheduler will be conjured to include a third case someplace our cluster.

The equivalent is valid if there are such a large number of pods running in the cluster at some random time. Along these lines, K8s are continually pushing towards that ideal state.

At last, we have, etcd, running as a conveyed configuration store. The Kubernetes state is put away here, and etcd enables qualities to be looked for changes. Think about this as the cerebrum's shared memory. Hub (in the past flunkies) In every hub, we have two or three components. The kublet interfaces with the Programming interface server to refresh state and to begin new workloads that have been conjured by the scheduler.

Kube-intermediary gives fundamental burden adjusting and coordinates traffic bound for specific services to the best possible case on the backend. See the Services segment later in this part.

At long last, we have some default pods, which run different foundation services for the hub. As we investigated quickly in the past part, the pods incorporate services for Domain Name System (DNS), logging, and case health checks.

The default case will run close by our planned pods on each hub.

Note that in v1.0, flunky was renamed to the hub; however, there are still leftovers of the term crony in a portion of the machine naming contents and documentation that exists on the Web.

Core construction

Presently, how about we plunge somewhat more profound and investigate a portion of the center deliberations Kubernetes gives.

These reflections will make it simpler to consider our applications and facilitate the weight of life cycle management, high accessibility, and booking.

Pods

Pods enable you to keep related containers close as far as the network and hardware foundation. Data can live approach the application, so processing can be managed without bringing about a high dormancy from network traversal.

Likewise, regular data can be put away on volumes that are shared between various containers.

While pods may run at least one container inside, the unit itself might be one of numerous that is running on a Kubernetes (flunky) hub. As we'll see, pods give us a consistent group of containers that we would then be able to repeat, calendar, and parity service endpoints over.

Unit model

We should investigate a unit in real life. We will turn up a Node.js application on the cluster. You'll require a GCE cluster running for this, Kubernetes and Container Operations, under the first cluster segment, if you don't as of now have once begun.

Presently, we should make a registry for our definitions. In this model, I will make an organizer in the/book-models subfolder under home registry.

$ mkdir book-models

$ disc book-models

$ mkdir 02_example

$ disc 02_example

Labels

Labels give us another degree of order, which turns out to be useful in terms of regular tasks and management. Like labels, labels can be utilized as the premise of service revelation just as a valuable grouping instrument for day to- day activities and management tasks.

Labels are merely straightforward key-esteem sets.

We will investigate labels more inside and out later in this part, on the whole, we will examine the staying two develops, services, and replication controllers.

The container's afterlife

As anybody in tasks can authenticate, disappointments happen regularly. Containers and pods can and will crash, become defiled, or perhaps simply get coincidentally close off by an awkward administrator looking around on one of the nodes. Strong arrangement and security rehearse like implementing the least benefit diminish a portion of these episodes; however, "automatic workload butcher occurs" and is just a reality of tasks.

Fortunately, Kubernetes gives two truly important develops to keep this solemn undertaking all cleaned up behind the window ornaments. Services and replication controllers give us the capacity to keep our applications running with little interference and easy recuperation.

Services

Services enable us to digest get away from the buyers of our applications.

Utilizing a solid endpoint, users and different projects can get to pods running on your cluster flawlessly.

K8s accomplishes this by ensuring that each hub in the cluster runs an intermediary named kube-intermediary. As the name recommends, kube-intermediary's main responsibility is to intermediary communication from a service endpoint back to the comparing unit that is running the real application.

The utilization of selectors and labels dictates enrollment in the service load adjusting pool. Pods with coordinating labels are added to the rundown of candidates where the service advances traffic. A virtual IP address and port are utilized as the passage point for the service, and traffic is then sent to a random unit on a target port characterized by either K8s or your definition file.

Updates to service definitions are observed and composed from the K8s cluster master and engendered to the kube-intermediary daemons running on each hub.

Tip

Right now, Kube-intermediary is running on the hub have itself. There are plans to containerize this and the kubelet as a matter of course later on.

Replication controllers

Replication controllers (RCs), as the name recommends, deal with the number of nodes that a unit and included container pictures run on. They guarantee that an occasion of a picture is being run with the specific number of duplicates.

As you start to operationalize your containers and pods, you'll need an approach to roll out updates, scale the number of duplicates running (both here and there), or essentially guarantee that in any event, one case of your stack is continually running. RCs make an elevated level component to ensure that things are operating effectively over the whole application and cluster.

RCs are just accused of guaranteeing that you have the ideal scale for your application. You characterize the number of case copies you need running and give it a format for how to make new pods. Much the same as services, we will utilize selectors and labels to characterize a case's enrollment in a replication controller.

Tip

Kubernetes doesn't require the exacting conduct of the replication controller. In certainty, version 1.1 has an occupation controller in beta that can be utilized for fleeting workloads, which enable occupations to be raced to a consummation state.

Chapter 6.
Kubernetes Cliene Libraries And Extensions

This chapter is going to attempt to demystify the several layers of networking operating in a Kubernetes cluster. Kubernetes is a very robust platform with a variety of intelligent designs to choose from. However, understanding how pods, container ports, networks, cluster IPs, node port, service networks, and host ports interact can be confusing.

For this reason, the whole process has been simplified in this book. We talk about these things mostly at work, cutting across all layers at once because something is broken and someone wants it fixed.

If you break it down and try to understand first how a single component works, it becomes clearer in a somewhat sophisticated way.

In order for us to keep things focused, I'm going to split the section into three parts. This first section will look at containers and pods. The second will examine and dissect services, which are the abstraction layer that allows pods to be ephemeral.

The last part will look at ingress and getting traffic to your pods from outside the cluster. A few disclaimers first. This section isn't intended to be a basic intro to containers, Kubernetes, or pods. Therefore, a basic familiarity with networking and IP address spaces will be helpful.

Pods

So, what is a pod? This isn't new to us, but a detail explanation will be given for clarity. A pod is made up of one or more containers placed side by side on the same host. Through configuration, they share a network stack and other resources, including volumes. Simply put the basic units which Kubernetes applications are constructed from are called pods.

What does "share a network stack" Really mean?

In more practical terms, it means that all the containers in a pod can reach each other on localhost. If I have two containers running at the same time; for example, nginx and scrapyd with the nginx listening on port 80, scrapyd can connect to it as http://localhost:80.

The Pod Network

That's really pretty cool, but one pod full of containers that can talk to each other does not get us a system.

For reasons that will become even clearer very soon when we shall be discussing services, with the Kubernetes' design it's a necessity that pods can communicate with each other whether or not they are running on the same localhost.

They must also be able to communicate with each other when they are on separate hosts. To see and understand how that happens, we need to step up a level and look at nodes in a cluster. This section will, unfortunately, contain some references to network routing and routes, a subject I realize all of humanity would prefer to avoid.

Finding a clearer, brief tutorial on IP routing is difficult, but if you want, a thorough review of Wikipedia's article on the topic isn't horrible.

Kubernetes cluster includes one or more nodes. A node is simply a host-system which can either be physical or virtual. A node has a container runtime and its dependencies (i.e., docker mostly) plus multiple Kubernetes system components, connected to a network making it possible to reach other nodes within the cluster.

Generally, you don't actually need to think about how this network functions. Whenever a pod communicates with another pod, it most often does so through the abstraction of service, which is a kind of software-defined proxy.

A network may need to be rerouted explicitly due to pod network addresses popping up in logs and during some set-up and debugging. For example, traffic leaving a Kubernetes pod bound for any address in the 10.0.0.0/8 range is not NAT'd by default.

Therefore, to communicate with services on a different private network in that particular range, setting up rules to route the packets back to the pods might be a necessity. Hopefully, this section of the book will help you make the right steps to make such scenarios work correctly.

In the first part of this section, I went over how Kubernetes allows pods running on separate cluster nodes to communicate with each other by using a combination of routing rules and virtual network devices. I explained that this is only possible if the sender knows the pod network IP address of the receiver.

If you aren't familiar with how pods communicate already, then it's worth a read before continuing.

Pod networking within a cluster is straightforward stuff, but by itself, it is insufficient to enable the creation of durable systems.

That's because pods in Kubernetes are ephemeral (transient). Although you are able to use a pod IP address as an endpoint, the address might change upon the next recreation of the pod. In some instances it might remain the same, but there is no guarantee.

There are many reasons which might cause this to happen.

You will probably have identified this as an old problem, and it has a standard solution: Just run the traffic through a reverse-proxy/load balancer.

Clients will connect to the proxy, and the proxy is responsible for maintaining a list of healthy servers to forward requests to. This will take us to a few requirements for the proxy:

- It must be durable and resistant to failure;
- Its must-have list of servers it can forward to;
- It must have a mechanism of knowing if a particular server is healthy and able to respond to requests.

This problem was solved in a classy way by the Kubernetes designers by improving on the basic capabilities of the platform. All three requirements are met starting with a resource type known as a service.

Services

Earlier I talked about a hypothetical cluster with two server pods and described how they are able to communicate across nodes. Now I will expound on that explaining how this happens while maintaining balance across a set of server pods, so that durability and independence are still possible in the operation of client pods.

A service is a type of Kubernetes resource that causes the configuration of a proxy, thereby allowing it to forward requests to a set of pods. The selector then determines which set of the pods receive the traffic by matching labels which were assigned to the pods during their creation. The service will then be assigned an IP address which will be able to accept requests on port 80 upon its successful creation.

It is better to use a hostname that resolves to the IP address even though the service IP can receive requests directly. A minor change to the client pod enables us to use the service name because Kubernetes offers an internal cluster DNS that resolves the service name:

After pod runs to completion, the output shows that the service forwarded the request to one of the server pods.

The client pod can continue to run, and each server pod will get approximately 50% of the requests. For those primarily interested in better understanding how this works, it is a good idea to start with the IP address assigned to our service.

The service networks

The IP that was assigned to the test service denotes an address on a network. Note though that this is not the same network as one that the pods are on.

It's also not the same with the private network the nodes are on, which will become clearer below. In order to retrieve this cluster property, you will need to use a provider-specific command because the pod network address range is not exposed via kubectl. This is also true of the service network address range.

The network that was specified by this address space is called the "service network." Every service that is of the type "ClusterIP" will be assigned an IP address on this network.

Like the pod-network, the service-network is actually virtual, but it differs from the pod-network in some amazing ways. Consider the pod-network address range 10.0.0.0/14. If you look closer at the hosts that make up the nodes in your cluster, listing bridges and interfaces you're going to see actual devices configured with addresses on this network.

These are really the virtual ethernet interfaces for each pod and the bridges that connect them to each other and the outside world.

Under no circumstances will you find any devices configured with addresses on the service network 10.3.240.0/20. You can closely examine the routing rules at the gateway that connects all the nodes, and you won't find any routes for this network.

The service network actually does not exist, at least not as connected interfaces. And as we saw above, whenever we issued a request to an IP on this network, somehow that request usually made it to our server pod running on the pod network.

When an interface is unable to deliver a packet to its destination due to the lack of a device with that specified address being present locally, the packet is forwarded to its upstream gateway through the IP networks' natural configuration of routes.

So, the first interface that locates the packets in this example is the virtual ethernet interface inside the client pod. That interface is located on the pod network 10.0.0.0/14 and doesn't know any devices with address 10.3.241.152.

It therefore forwards the packet to the bridge cbr0, which is its gateway. Bridges are just dumb and will only pass traffic back and forth, so the bridge sends the packet on to the host-node ethernet interface.

The host-node in this example, the ethernet interface is on the network 10.100.0.0/24, and it doesn't know any devices with the address 10.3.241.152 either. The packet would, therefore, be forwarded out to this interface's gateway, as shown in the drawing (the top-level router). Instead, what really happens is that the packet is snagged in flight and redirected to one of the live server pods.

When I started working with Kubernetes three years ago most of the things explained above seemed pretty magical to me, and I don't expect you to fully understand this narrative especially if you are just starting Kubernetes.

The mysterious software known as Kube-proxy allowed all my clients to connect to an address with no interface associated with it. The packets then popped out at the correct place in the cluster.

Kube-proxy

Like everything in Kubernetes, a service is simply a resource that explains how to configure some bit of software to do something. In fact, the service affects. The behavior and configuration of many components in the cluster, including the very important Kube-proxy, are affected by the service. Based on the name of this proxy, many of you might already have an idea of what this does, but it's not quite the same as a typical reverse-proxy like haproxy or linkerd.

The typical behavior of a proxy is to pass traffic between clients and servers over two open connections. Clients can connect inbound to a service port, and the proxy connects outbound to a server. Since all proxies of this nature run in user space, this means that packets are marshaled into users pace and back to kernel space on every trip through the proxy. Initially, the Kube-proxy was implemented as just such a user-space proxy, but with a twist. A proxy requires an interface, both to listen on for client connections, and to use to connect to back-end servers. The only interfaces that are available on a node are either

1. the host's ethernet interface; or

2. the virtual ethernet interfaces on the pod network.

Why not consider using an address on one of those networks?

I don't have any internal workings or knowledge; however, with pods and nodes being ephemeral entities in the cluster, it is evident that in so doing, the routing rules for those networks designed to serve these pods and nodes would have been complicated. Services clearly required their own, stable, non-conflicting network address space, and a system of virtual IPs makes the most sense.

However, as we have noted, there are no actual devices on this network. This, therefore, means that it is not possible to open a connection through an interface that doesn't exist or listen on a port. You can, however, utilize a virtual network in routing rules, firewall filters, etc.

Kubernetes gets past this hurdle using a feature of the Linux kernel called net-filter, and a user space interface that's known as "IP-Tables." If you want to read and learn more about it, the Netfilter page is a good place to start.

Here the TL:dr: Netfilter is a rules-based packet processing engine. It actually runs in kernel-space and gets a look at every packet at various points in its life cycle. It matches packets against the rules, and when it finds a rule that matches, it takes the specified action. It can redirect the packet to an alternate destination thereby making it a kernel space-proxy.

Multi-tenancy in Kubernetes

Sharing a Cluster with Multi-Users

Kubernetes can be organizing for hundreds of users. Rather than providing a cluster for each user, we can decide to take a different approach by simply implementing multi-tenancy on a single Kubernetes cluster. This section will describe the different steps that are involved to properly set up a multi-tenant Kubernetes cluster readily available for use by multiple developers in a lab session.

Labs are great, but, one of the biggest challenges is to ensure that the lab environment is properly organized and efficiently set up for all the participant. If not, your contributors might get irritated or frustrated, even before you have a chance to get to the interesting part of your lab.

Also, as an organizer, you want to make sure that you create an enabling environment that will allow all the contributors to dive into the good stuff as fast as humanly feasible. And trust me, when you have over 100 participants, with different skill levels as well as different hardware, the initial lab set up can take a while if it's not made simple.

And so, for a Kubernetes "hands-on" lab, most developers are on the lookout for the best solution to have an easy Kubernetes lab environment.

Some will even play with the idea of installing minikube for all the participants and ask them to start a Kubernetes mono node cluster, thanks to it. But they were afraid to face "unusual" laptop enterprise configuration with strict firewall, antivirus issue or other security setups that would block the instantiation of VMs.

This is why most developers decided to search for another better solution, for instance, using a managed Kubernetes Cluster like GKE (Google Kontainer Engine). Representation as or by an instance is easily achieved. Except in the case where you are creating individual clusters for each participant, it will cost a few cents if you start the cluster only for the time of your lab.

Hence, the reason for investigating the configuration of clusters for multi-tenant usage where each user gets one namespace and one authentication access.

This multi-tenant cluster configuration for the lab is the occasion to come back on several isolations and security features offered natively by Kubernetes.

Isolation

This not actually a new thing, by splitting usage of several users in different Namespace in the same Kubernetes cluster the users can be perfectly isolated. In addition to the Namespace technique, a Quota resource can be created and associated with each namespace in order to avoid the possibility to have one user starving all cluster resources. You also need to force the user to set limits on Pod definition (memory and CPU).

To achieve this employ the aid of Admission Controller alongside the creation of a "Limit Range" resource for each namespace. By creating this "Limit Range" resource, the default limit values are added in the Pod definition if the user didn't set them initially.

SUMMARY: TL; DR: Namespace + Quota + LimitRange = Ideal Isolation

Authentication

Several Kubernetes plugins or extensions like Correos dex already exist for managing the user authentication. But all the solutions that we found required to have also an authentication provider behind; And since we don't want to lose time during a Lab to ask everyone to create a user on a specific provider like GitHub, an LDAP server---- we looked at another solution.

The native solution for authentication is the "Service Account." When you create a new "Service Account" resource, the k8s controller automatically creates an associated secret containing security certificates. These certificates can be used to communicate with the API server, but also the secret contains a token that can be used as a "bearer authentication token" in any HTTP request for the same purpose.

This token can actually be used in a Kubernetes config file inside a "user" authentication information.

The authentication problem is already solved; we will create a dedicated Service Account in each namespace lab, then generate and distribute to each user a kubeconfig file like the previous example.

Permission

Individual users should have access only to the resources created in his dedicated Namespace. Access means the possibility to list, have the resources but also create and update those resources. For this kind of problem, Kubernetes implements the concept of RBAC that allows a Kubernetes cluster-admin to assign fine-grained permission on each resource kind to each user or group. By default, when the RBAC is activated on your Kubernetes cluster, a Service Account has no permission to access resources information through the API server.

A "Role" resource outlining a set of rules denoting user permission on a specific set of resources are created to accurately set the user permissions inside an individual user's namespace. Then the association between the Role, the Service Account, and the Namespace is done thanks to a Role-Binding resource.

In this case, the Role and Role-Binding will allow any interaction between the user (Service Account) and the API-Server as long as the resources that are targeted belong to the user's namespace.

Kubernetes Dashboard access

The Kubernetes dashboard or interface is a great tool for new users to see and navigate between Kubernetes resources. So, for a Hands-on lab, this is very useful, and the user should be encouraged to use this dashboard, but it required an extra configuration to allow this in our previous permission configuration.

By following the instructions on the dashboard install guide, it is installed in a specific Namespace "Kube-system." In order for individual users to access this UI, they will need to create local HTTP proxy to the API-server by using the "kubectl proxy" command. In order to properly use this API-Server service proxy feature, the user-specific permission on the "services/proxy" sub-resource in the "Kube-system" namespace.

Chapter 7. Logging

When you are using monitoring functions, then you can easily dig out components that show whether your system has failed or if there is a problem you might have overlooked. However, in many cases, you might not be able to discover the root cause of the problem.

This is why you have the process of logging.

Let us take a simple example. Imagine that you have run a program that is going to produce the sum of all the numbers from 1 to 100. You know that the result is 5,050. However, as you were monitoring the process, you realized that the program skipped the number 50.

You know that there was an error in that process. But when you get the result, you notice that the final number is 4,900. You know that the program has omitted the number 50, but you don't know what other numbers were removed and for that matter, why those numbers have been excluded. You then go to the log and notice where the errors have happened and also why they occurred.

The process of logging allows you to refine your program so that it makes fewer and fewer errors in the future. Think of it this way: monitoring allows you to effectively look at the present situation of the program. However, logging allows you go back to the beginning if you would like to and check for any inconsistencies.

Generally, there are two important posts to a logging system. You have the logging agent and then the backend.

The logging agent is a layer that is responsible for gathering information and dispatching the information to the backend. When the information reaches the backend, then all the logs are saved. One of the most challenging parts of creating logs is for Kubernetes to determine how to gather logs from various containers and then transfer them to a centralized backend. Thankfully, there is a solution for that.

The most efficient method of creating logs is to assign logging agents for each and every node and configuring them in such a way that they forward all the information to one destination. To do so, we can create what is known as a sidecar container.

A sidecar container is a special utility entity. It does not perform any actions on its own, but actually supports the main container. This process is useful to us, as we can simply create a sidecar container to deal with the logs of each container within a pod.

That way, we do not have to worry about managing each and every log file since that is automatically done by the sidecar container. Here is a script that you can use for such a sidecar container:

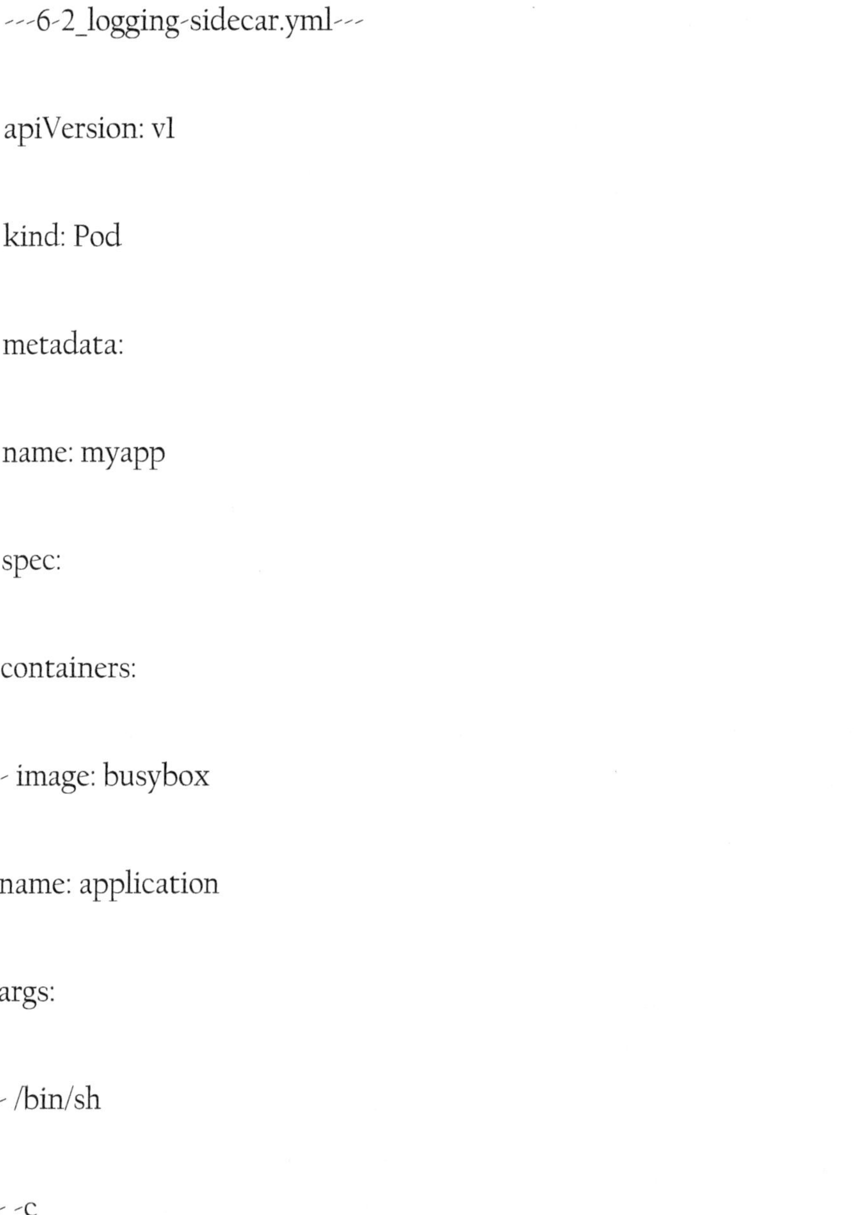

```
---6-2_logging-sidecar.yml---

apiVersion: v1

kind: Pod

metadata:

name: myapp

spec:

containers:

- image: busybox

name: application

args:

- /bin/sh

- -c
```

```
- >
while true; do
echo "$(date) INFO hello" >> /var/log/myapp.log;
sleep 1;
done
volumeMounts:
- name: log
mountPath: /var/log
- name: sidecar
image: busybox
args:
- /bin/sh
- -c
- tail -fn+1 /var/log/myapp.log
```

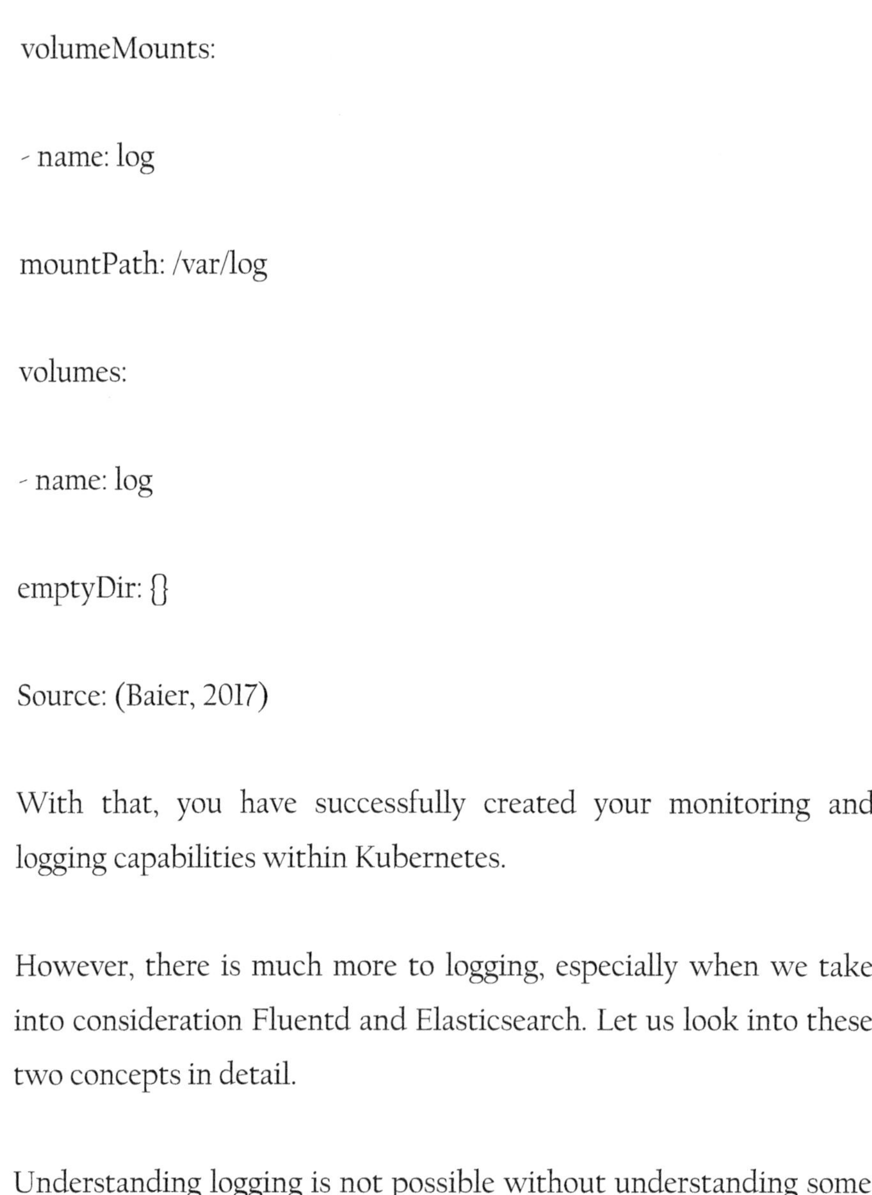

```
volumeMounts:
- name: log
mountPath: /var/log
volumes:
- name: log
emptyDir: {}
```

Source: (Baier, 2017)

With that, you have successfully created your monitoring and logging capabilities within Kubernetes.

However, there is much more to logging, especially when we take into consideration Fluentd and Elasticsearch. Let us look into these two concepts in detail.

Understanding logging is not possible without understanding some of the basic components that comprise logging.

The first component that we need to look at is stdout.

The stdout or standard output is the default file descriptor that is used by a particular process in order to produce an output. A file descriptor refers to a unique number that identifies a particular file in your operating system.

For example, your Word software might have the file descriptor of 12 and MS PowerPoint might have the file descriptor iofg 567. Each program has its own number and this is used by the operating system whenever it would like to access that program or provides its location to another software.

Let's take an example here. You might have heard of the popular file extracting software WinRAR. Your operating system might give WinRAR a file descriptor of 56. Now let's imagine that you have a compressed file that you would like to extract.

When you use WinRAR to extract your file, then your OS lets the file know that it should be looking for the program with the file descriptor 56. Think of file descriptors as the number plates on a car; each number lets you know which car you are looking for.

Your individual containers utilize stdout in order to create output. It is this output that we need to be concerned about since it contains all the details of the activity performed by the particular container.

Another component that we need to look at is stderr. This functions similar to stdout, but the main purpose of the stderr is to write error messages.

We now have two different output methods, the stdout and stderr. The easiest way to record logs is to create two sidecar containers for the two methods of recording output, where one method (stdout) handles the activity while the other (stderr) handles the error.

Here is an example of an activity that will result in a container creating a logging entry to stdout:

apiVersion: vl

kind: Pod

metadata:

name: example

spec:

containers:

- name: example

image: busybox

args: [/bin/sh, -c, 'while true; do echo $(date); sleep 1; done']

Source: (Baier, 2017)

In order to check the logs of that container, you simply have to use the log container-name command.

So far, so good. Now we get into the details.

Fluentd

Your biggest problem is not the log itself. After all, we just looked at how you can create a sidecar container to manage your logs. Your biggest challenge is to gather the logs from hundreds of different sources and unify them, a task that is much more complicated than it sounds. If you are a system administrator, then you are going to be constantly dealing with complex sets of procedures to analyze and parse service logs. Add to this the fact that you are not just going to be utilizing applications on a PC or laptop browser, but making sure that the application runs smoothly on mobile devices and you have so many different areas to look at. It reaches a point where it is physically impossible for you to start extracting logs from everywhere.

In such scenarios, you need a platform that provides you the below benefits when it comes to logging:

- The platform is a high-performing one
- There is minimal data loss
- The system is reliable

This is where Fluentd comes into play. Fluentd is a platform that allows you to gather a high-performing layer for your container that allows it to assist you with the logging process.

One of the unique characteristics of Fluentd is that it structures data in such a way that it becomes easy to unify all the various aspects of log data. It can easily collect, filter, buffer, and then create an output for the data logs from multiple sources and components.

In order to install Fluentd, your first step is to download the msi file that you can find right here: https://td-agent-package-browser.herokuapp.com/3/windows

Once you have installed the msi file, you are going to spot this program: Td-agent Command Prompt. Activate it by double-clicking the program icon.

In the next step, you will notice a prompt. Enter the below command:

› fluentd -c etc\td-agent\td-agent.conf

Execute the above command and then launch another Td-agent Command Prompt. In the second prompt, you have to type this command:

› echo {"message":"hello"} | fluent-cat test.event

For the next step, we have to make sure that you register the program to your Windows so that it can use your system as a permanent process. In order to do so, run the Td-agent Command Prompt again. This time, enter the below commands:

› fluentd --reg-winsvc i

› fluentd --reg-winsvc-fluentdopt '-c C:/opt/td-agent/etc/td-agent/td-agent.conf -o C:/opt/td-agent/td-agent.log'

Source: (Baier, 2017)

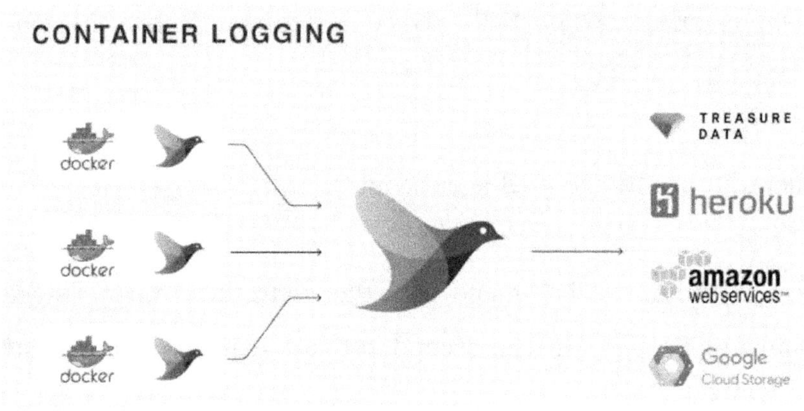

Fluentd takes logs from Docker and then stores them in your chosen cloud service platform such as GCE or AWS.

For the next step, you need to navigate to the Control Panel in the Windows menu. Head over to System and Security. Then you have to navigate to Administrative Tools and finally click on Services.

You will be able to see an option that says Fluentd Window Service. Open the application and then click the option Start. You should be able to see the below at this point, which shows that you have successfully installed the application:

› net start fluentd winsvc

The Fluentd Windows Service service is starting.

The Fluentd Windows Service service was started successfully.

For the final step, we are going back to Td-agent Command Prompt. Once you open the prompt, you are going to update the application. Simply enter the below command and you are good to go:

› fluent-gem install fluent-plugin-xyz --version=XXX

If you would like to know the latest version of the application, then you simply have to visit this link: https://docs.fluentd.org/quickstart/update-from-v0.12

Once you have completed the installation, Fluentd will then start the logging process.

Elasticsearch

Think about this scenario.

You have compiled large volumes of data. This volume keeps increasing the more logs you create. Imagine that one day, you decide to examine the data because you discovered a problem in your application.

Wouldn't that be such a cumbersome job to do now that you have so much data to sift through? You can't possibly go through each and every piece of data hoping to find what you are looking for.

Wouldn't it be convenient if you had a search function where you simply have to enter a value and you are taken to that data?

This is where Elasticsearch becomes your preferred tool for search-related functions. Regular database management systems are not meant for performing complex searches or running full-text queries.

In order to use elasticsearch, you do not require a complicated installation procedure. Simple head over to their web page and download the latest version. You can start off with a trial mode and then shift to a full version if you feel like it is something you might use for the long term.

Simply head over to https://www.elastic.co/downloads/ to find the file and download it onto your system.

While we are adding new components to our database, it is also important to maintain its integrity. This is where the concept of security comes into place.

Chapter 8. The Intricacies Of This Management Plane In Kubernetes

Controllers

The Kubernetes controller supervisor is a daemon that embeds the control that is heart Kubernetes was shipped with by loops. In robotics and automation, a control loop is a loop that modulates a system's condition.

This is one instance of a control loop: a thermostat at a space. When you place the desired condition, the room temperature is your condition that is present by turning the equipment off or on the thermostat functions to bring the condition to the condition.

Kubernetes runs a set of controls that take good care of tasks that are routine to make sure the state of the bunch matches with the state that is observed.

Each control is responsible for a source in the world. This page collects resources; including information regarding node controls replication controls, and also the Kubernetes control supervisor.

Controls are control loops that observe your's condition, bunch, request, or then make changes. Each control attempts to maneuver the bunch state nearer to the state.

Controller pattern

A control monitors kind that is one Kubernetes source. These items possess a field that reflects the state that is desired. The control s for that source accounts for producing the present state come nearer to this desired state. The control might carry the action out itself in Kubernetes; messages will be sent by control into the API server, which has useful side effects.

You will see examples of this below. All controls are packed and sent in one to decrease the daemon called complexity kube-controller-manager. The simplest implementation of control is a loop:

Controller components

There are two primary constituents of a controller: operate queue and informer/sharedinformer. Informer/sharedinformer watches for changes on the present condition of Kubernetes items and sends events to workqueue where events are subsequently popped up by employee (s) to process.

Informer

The role of a controller would be to see objects for the state, and the state sends directions to produce the state to be like the state. To retrieve the data of an object, the control sends a petition. But repeatedly data from the API server may get pricey. So, record multiple times to items in code, and to get, Kubernetes programmers wind up using the cache that has been supplied from the library.

The controller does not wish to send orders. It cares about occasions once the item was created, altered, or deleted. The client-go library provides the listwatcher interface which performs the first list and begins an eye on a specific source:

Lw:= cache. Newlistwatchfromclient (

Customer,

&{V1. Podv1. Pod undefined,

Api. Namespaceall,

Fieldselector)

All these items are absorbed in informer. A general arrangement of an informer is clarified below:

Shop, controller:= cache. Newinformer{

&{Cache. Listwatchcache. Listwatch undefined,

&{V1. Podv1. Pod undefined,

Resyncperiod,

{Cache. Resourceeventhandlerfuncscache. Resourceeventhandlerfuncs undefined,

Although Informer Has Not Been Utilized Much From The Recent Kubernetes (Rather Sharedinformer Is Utilized, Which i'll Explain Later), It's Still A Vital Concept To Comprehend, Particularly Once You Would Like To Compose A Customized Controller. T

He following are the three designs utilized to assemble the informer:

Listwatcher

Listwatcher is a combination of also a watch along with a listing function purpose for a source in a namespace. This also assists the control focus just it needs to look at. The area selector is a sort of filter that narrows the result, such as a controller would like to regain resources matching a field of looking for a source. The arrangement of a listwatcher is clarified below:

- cache. ListWatch undefined

Resource Event Handler

Resource event handler is where the control manages notifications for modifications on a specific source:

Kind resourceeventhandlerfuncs struct {

Addfunc func (obj {interfaceinterface undefined)

Updatefunc func (oldobj, newobj {interfaceinterface undefined)

Deletefunc func (obj undefined

- AddFunc is known as there is a resource created.

- When a present source is modified, updateFunc is called. The older it is this resource's last condition. If a re-synchronization occurs, updateFunc is called, and it has called if nothing changes.

- DeleteFunc is known as a present source, is deleted. It will get the last condition of this source (if it's known). It will get an object of type DeletedFinalStateUnknown. This sometimes happens whether the watch deletes the occasion and is shut, and the deletion doesn't be noticed by the control.

Resyncperiod

Resyncperiod defines the control fires the updatefunc and then goes through all things. This provides the condition to be occasionally verified by a type of configuration and make it. It is extremely helpful. In the case, actions, or upgrades failed. In the event the interval time is brief, if you construct a custom made control, then you have to be cautious using the CPU load.

SharedInformer

The informer a cache of some set of tools used alone. However, a package is of control caring and running about types of resources. This usually means that there'll be an overlap -. In cases like this, the sharedinformer helps to produce a single cache among controls.

This implies cached resources will not be replicated, and the memory overhead of this system is decreased, by doing so. Every sharedinformer generates a watch irrespective of the number of events are being read by customers that are downstream in the informer. This lessens the load on the server.

This is typical for the kube-controller-manager, which includes many controls. The sharedinformer has supplied hooks to get notifications of updating, adding, and deleting a specific resource.

Additionally, it provides convenience functions for ascertaining when a cache is primed and accessing caches. This saves us relations contrary to the API server, replicate deserialization prices controller-side replicate serialization costs server-side, and replicate caching prices controller-side.

Lw:= cache. Newlistwatchfromclient (. . .)

Shsharedinformer: cacache. Newsharedinformerw, &ap{i. Podundefined,|API. Pod undefined resyncperiod)

Workqueue

The sharedinformer cannot monitor where every control is left up to (because it is shared), so the controller has to supply its own queuing and retrying mechanism (if needed). Therefore resource event handlers place things on a labor queue that is per-consumer. Every time a source the resource event handler, changes places a secret.

A Keynes the structure / unless it is vacant, then it is only. By doing this, events are dropped by essential so every consumer can use employee (s) to soda up key, and this function isareone sequentially. This will ensure that no two employees will operate on exactly the key at precisely the same moment.

The job queue is supplied from the library in client-go/util/workqueue. There are lots of sorts of queues such as queue, a queue that is timed, and the queue.

The next is an example for producing a rate-limiting lineup:

Queue::work queue. Newratelimitingqueue (rk ququeue. Defaultcontrollerratelimiter)

Workqueue supplies convenience functions to handle keys. The next figure explains the kekeylife-cycle in workqueue:

In the case of collapse when calculating an event, the control calls for the adaddratelimited (function toto? Push it is crucial back to the job queue to operate on using several retries. If the approach is effective, the key could be removed from the job queue by calling the foforget (function. But the job queue stops from monitoring the history of this function.

To take out the event entirely, the control has to activate the dodone (function. Hence the job can handle notifications. However, the question is, when should control start employees? There are two reasons that the control must wait before the cache is synchronized to attain the newest conditions:

- Before the cache has completed synchronizing List, each of the tools will be wrong.
- The cache/queue will collapses in the version multiple updates into a source. It has to wait until the cache gets idle before processing things to prevent work.

The pseudo-code under clarifies that clinic:

Controller. Informer = cache. Newsharedinformer)

Controller. Queue = woworkqueue. Newratelimitingqueueoworkqueue. Defaultcontrollerratelimiter)

Controller. Informer. Run(stopch)

If !Cacache. Waitforcachesynctopch, cocontroller. Hassynched/p›

Undefined

// Now begin processing

Cocontroller. Runworker (/p› control through the API server

The work controller is a good illustration of a Kubernetes controller that is built-in. By interacting with the bunch, API server controllers manage the condition. Job is a Kubernetes source that runs maybe pods, or on the pod, to conduct a job and then cease.

(After scheduled, pod objects become a part of this desirable condition for a kusublet

Whenever the work controller sees a new task, it makes certain that in your audience, the cutlets a pair of nodes are currently conducting pods' amount to get the job done. It does not operate containers or any pods. The work controller informs the API server to eliminate or to make pods.

Other elements in the management airplane act on the new data (you will find fresh pods to program and operate), and at some point, the job is finished. Once you create a new job, the desirable state is for this particular job finished. The work controller makes the state for this job be closer to a condition that is preferred: that the job is nearer to completion, generating you desired for that job. Controllers upgrade.

For instance: once the job is completed to get work, the work controller upgrades that job object to indicate it finished. (This is somewhat like how some thermostats tuto turn light off to signify that your area is currently in the temperature you place).

Immediate control

By comparison, a few, with job controls, will need to make adjustments. For instance, if you use a control loop to be certain that there are nodes in your cluster, control needs something to prepare nodes when required.

Controllers that interact with states find their condition then speak directly to bring the condition.

(There really is a controller that leaves the nodes in your cluster.

Desired versus the present state

Kubernetes takes a cloud-native will manage change and perspective of systems. Your audience could be shifting at any given stage as the work occurs, and control loops mechanically fix failures. It follows that your audience never reaches a steady condition. Your audience is running and ready to produce modifications; it is irrelevant whether the state isn't stable or is.

Layout

As a tenet of its layout, Kubernetes uses plenty of controls that every handle a specific facet of this cluster state. Most commonly, a specific control loop (control) uses one particular type of source as its preferred state and contains a different sort of source it manages to create this desirable condition occur. It is helpful to have controls than one control loops. Controllers may fail.

Therefore Kubernetes was made to permit that. As an example, a control for jobs monitors job items (to find fresh work) and pod thing (to conduct the jobs, then to observe if the job is completed). In cases like this, jobs, whereas the work controller generates pods, are created by something.

Notice:

There can be many controllers that upgrade or make the kind of object. Behind the scenes, Kubernetes controls are certain they focus on the sources connected to their resources. As an instance, you may have jobs and deployments; pods are both created by those.

The job control doesn't delete the pods your deployment generated since there's data (tags) the controls can use to inform people pods apart.

Ways of conducting controllers

Kubernetes comes. These controls give significant core behaviors.

Job control and the deployment control are examples of controls that come as part of Kubernetes itself ("built-in" controls). Kubernetes lets a control airplane that is resilient runs so that if some of those controls were to fail, a different portion of the control airplane would take the work over.

You can find controls that operate to extend Kubernetes. Or, if you would like, it is possible to write control yourself. It's possible to conduct your control or to Kubernetes . What fits best depends on what that controller does.

Kubernetes Control Plane

The Kubernetes control plane's areas, like the Kubernetes master and sublet procedures, govern Kubernetes , and your audience to communicate. The control plane keeps a listing of all the Kubernetes objects and conducts control loops to handle those objects' states. At any time, the controller loops of the control plane work to generate the condition is matched by the state of the items in the machine which you supplied and will react to changes from the audience.

By way of example, when you use the Kubernetes API to make you, a deployment provide a new state for the machine. The Kubernetes control plane documents that thing production and carries by beginning the software and scheduling them to cluster nodes creating the cluster state matches the state.

If you are considering conducting a Kubernetes system, different cloud surroundings, you need to check out exactly what bob wise and his staff at samsung sds phone"control plane engineering. "

During his keynote in cloudnativecon year, he explained the idea of constructing nodes to guarantee uptime and functionality across clouds, creates a setup that's readily scaled from the clusterops staff, and cover audience requirements. "[Should you think] the thought of Kubernetes as a fantastic way to run the same systems on several clouds, multiple people clouds, and several sorts of personal clouds is important, and if you care about this, you take care of control airplane technology," wise explained.

By focusing on the coating, sharing functionality and setting. Information with all the community, wise said Kubernetes deployments that were bigger could become more manageable and simpler. "among the things we are attempting to foster, attempting to construct some tooling and make some donation around is a means for members of their community to catch their audience configuration, what they've such as things like placing of audience, can catch that, ditch that, and catch export and that it for sharing, and to shoot performance information with that audience and do exactly the very same," wise explained. "

The aim here would be, across a vast selection of conditions, to have the ability to begin to compare notes throughout the community."

For the job his staff and wise have done, four are involved by the control airplane components that sit to be things operate despite nodes and equipment failure.

The control plane contains:

- An API Server around front end by which each of the elements interacts,
- A Scheduler to assign components,

- The ETCD, a distributed database program in which bunch state is preserved, and

- A Controller Supervisor, that's the house for embedded control loops such as copy places, deployments, tasks, etc. .

The best way to conduct the machine that it's some degree of allocation automation is via Kubernetes self-hosting," wise said. But that needs some"catchy bootstrapping" to construct it. In the long run, it is well worth it if you are running an audience.

"The notion here is it is a system completely operating as Kubernetes items," that he said. "You've got this frequent operation collection. It is likely to create scaling. . . "a one-piece that is better not to attempt to construct on your own would be a load balancer a bottleneck to the computer system.

Wise said with the load balancer of a cloud provider is the easiest, and in the long run, likely the ideal solution. "This load balancer, this is a crucial part of the overall system availability and performance," wise explained. "The cloud suppliers have placed enormous investment to great options.

Use them and be joyful. "It is worth the setup drift that occurs between multiple deployments," wise continued. “Would also say again you've got on-premises, and you are attempting to perform deployments, and you currently have these load balancers they then operate nicely, they are pretty straightforward to configure generally.

The settings that Kubernetes demands support are not complex. If you've got them, use them to be glad, but I would not suggest going and purchasing those appliances. "

Chapter 9. Cluster Federation

This part will examine the new organization capacities and how to utilize them to deal with different groups crosswise over cloud suppliers. We will likewise cover the united variant of the center builds. We will walk you through combined Deployments, ReplicaSets, ConfigMaps, and Events.

This part will talk about the following themes:

Federating bunches

Federating different groups

Inspecting and controlling assets over different groups

Launching assets over different groups

Introduction to organization

While organization is still new in Kubernetes, it lays the preparation for the exceptionally looked for cross-cloud supplier arrangement.

Using alliance, we can run different Kubernetes groups on-premise and in at least one open cloud suppliers and oversee applications utilizing the whole arrangement of all our authoritative assets.

This begins to create a way for avoiding cloud supplier lock-in and profoundly accessible sending that can put application servers in numerous bunches and take into account correspondence to different administrations situated in single points among our united groups.

We can improve detachment on blackouts at a specific supplier or geographic area while providing more prominent adaptability for scaling and utilizing all out infrastructure.

At present, the league plane backings these assets (ConfigMap, DaemonSets, Deployment, Events, Ingress, Namespaces, ReplicaSets, Secrets, and Services). Note that league and its parts are in alpha and beta periods of discharge, so usefulness may in any case be somewhat touchy.

Setting up league

While we can utilize the bunch we had running for the remainder of the models, I would profoundly prescribe that you start new. The default naming of the bunches and settings can be risky for the organization system.

Note that the - bunch setting and - mystery name banners are there to assist you with working around the default naming, yet for first-time alliance, it can even now be confusing and not exactly clear.

Henceforth, starting crisp is the means by which we will stroll through the models in this section. Either utilize new and separate cloud supplier (AWS and/or GCE) records or tear down the present bunch and reset your Kubernetes control condition by running the following commands:

$kubectl config unset settings

$kubectl config unset groups

Twofold watch that nothing is recorded using the following commands:

$kubectl config get-settings

$kubectl config get-bunches

Next, we will need to get the kubefed command on our way and make it executable. Explore back to the envelope where you have the Kubernetes download extricated. The kubefed command is situated in the/kubernetes/customer/bin envelope.

Run the following commands to get in the bin organizer and change the execution authorizations:

$sudo cp kubernetes/customer/bin/kubefed/usr/nearby/bin

$sudo chmod +x/usr/nearby/bin/kubefed

Settings

Settings are utilized by the Kubernetes control plane to keep confirmation and bunch setup put away for various groups. This enable us to get to and deal with numerous bunches available from the equivalent kubectl.

You can generally observe the settings accessible with the get-settings command that we utilized before.

New bunches for alliance

Again, ensure you explore to any place Kubernetes was downloaded and move into the bunch sub-organizer:

$ compact disc kubernetes/group/

In the first place, we will create the AWS bunch. Note that we are adding a situation variable named OVERRIDE_CONTEXT that will enable us to set the setting name to something that follows the DNS naming standards. DNS is a basic segment for organization as it enables us to do cross-group revelation and administration correspondence.

This is significant in a unified reality where groups might be in different server farms and even suppliers.

Run these commands to create your AWS group:

$export KUBERNETES_PROVIDER=aws

$export OVERRIDE_CONTEXT=awsk8s

$./kube-up.sh

Next, we will create a GCE group, by and by using the OVERRIDE_CONTEXT condition variable:

$export KUBERNETES_PROVIDER=gce

$export OVERRIDE_CONTEXT=gcek8s

$./kube-up.sh

In the event that we investigate our settings now, we will see both the awsk8s and the gcek8s that we just created. The star before gcek8s means that it's the place kubectl is at present pointing and executing against:

$ kubectl config get-settings

Initializing the league control plane

Since we have two bunches, we should set up the alliance control plane in the GCE group. To begin with, we'll have to ensure that we are in the GCE setting, and then we will initialize the alliance control plane:

$ kubectl config use-setting gcek8s

$kubefed init ace control - have group context=gcek8s - dns-zone-name="mydomain.com"

The preceding command creates another setting only for league called ace control. It utilizes the gcek8s bunch/setting to have the league segments, (for example, API server and controller). It accept GCE DNS as the organizations DNS administration.

You'll have to refresh dns-zone-name with a domain addition you oversee.

As a matter of course, the DNS supplier is GCE. You can utilize - dns-provider="aws-route53" to set it to AWS route53; be that as it may, out of the crate execution still has issues for some clients.

On the off chance that we check our settings by and by we will presently observe three settings:

$ kubectl config get-settings

How about we ensure we have all the organization segments running before we continue. The league control plane uses the alliance system namespace. Utilize the kubectl get cases command with the namespace determined to screen the advancement. When you see two API server cases and one controller unit you ought to be set:

$ kubectl get cases - namespace=federation-system

Since we have the league parts set fully operational, we should change to that setting for the subsequent stages:

$ kubectl config use-setting expert control

Adding bunches to the league system

Since we have our league control plane we can add the bunches to the alliance system. To begin with, we will join the GCE group and then the AWS bunch:

$kubefed join gcek8s - have bunch context=gcek8s - mystery name=fed-mystery gce

$kubefed join awsk8s - have bunch context=gcek8s - mystery name=fed-mystery aws

Unified assets

Unified assets enable us to convey over different groups and/or locales. As of now, adaptation 1.5 of Kubernetes bolster various center asset types in the alliance API, including ConfigMap, DaemonSets, Deployment, Events, Ingress, Namespaces, ReplicaSets, Secrets, and Services.

How about we investigate a Federated Deployment that will enable us to plan units crosswise over both

AWS and GCE:

apiVersion: augmentations/v1beta1

kind: Deployment

metadata:

name: hub js-convey

marks:

name: hub js-convey

spec:

imitations: 3

format:

metadata:

marks:

name: hub js-convey

spec:

containers:

- name: hub js-convey

picture: jonbaier/case scaling:latest ports:

- containerPort: 80

Listing 9-1. hub js-convey fed.yaml

Create this organization with the following command:

$ kubectl create - f hub js-convey fed.yaml

Presently how about we have a go at listing the cases from this organization:

$ kubectl get units

We should see a message like the preceding one portrayed. This is on the grounds that we are as yet using the ace control or organization setting, which doesn't itself run cases. We will, in any case, see the organization in the alliance plane and in the event that we inspect the occasions we will see that the sending was in certainty created on both our united groups:

$ kubectl get arrangements

$ kubectl portray arrangements hub js-convey

We should see something like the following. Notice that the Events: segment shows arrangements in both our GCE and AWS settings:

We can likewise observe the combined occasions using the following command:

```
$ kubectl get occasions
```

It might pause for a minute for every one of the three cases to run. When that occurs, we can change to each bunch setting and see a portion of the units on each. Note that we would now be able to utilize get units since we are on the individual groups and not on the control plane:

```
$kubectl config use-setting awsk8s

$kubectl get units

$kubectl config use-setting gcek8s

$kubectl get units
```

We should see the three units spread over the groups with two on one and a third on the other. Kubernetes has spread it over the group with no manual intervention. Any cases that bomb will be restarted, yet now we have the additional repetition of two cloud suppliers.

Unified designs

In present day software advancement, it isn't unexpected to isolate setup factors from the application code itself. In this manner it is simpler to make updates to support URLs, accreditations, regular ways, and so on. Having these qualities in outer arrangement files implies we can undoubtedly refresh setup without rebuilding the whole application.

This partition takes care of the initial issue, yet obvious transportability comes when you can expel the reliance from the application totally. Kubernetes offers a design store for precisely this reason. ConfigMaps are straightforward builds that store key-esteem sets.

Kubernetes likewise bolsters Secrets for increasingly touchy arrangement information. You can utilize the model there in both single bunches or on the league control plane as we are demonstrating with ConfigMaps here.

How about we investigate a model that will enable us to store some setup and then expend it in different cases. The following listings will work for both combined and single bunches, however we will continue using a united arrangement for this model.

The ConfigMap kind can be created using strict qualities, level files and registries, and finally

YAML definition files. The following listing is a YAML definition file:

apiVersion: vl

kind: ConfigMap

metadata:

name: my-application-config

namespace: default

information:

backend-service.url: my-backend-administration

Listing 9-2: configmap-fed.yaml

Allows first switch back to our alliance plane:

$ kubectl config use-setting expert control

Presently, create this listing with the following command:

$ kubectl create - f configmap-fed.yaml

How about we show the configmap object that we just created. The - o yaml banner encourages us show the full information:

$ kubectl get configmap my-application-config - o yaml

Since we have a ConfigMap object, how about we fire up a united ReplicaSet that can utilize the ConfigMap. This will create copies of cases over our bunch that can get to

the ConfigMap object. ConfigMaps can be gotten to through condition factors or mount volumes. This model will utilize a mount volume that gives an envelope chain of command and the files for each key with the substance representing the qualities:

apiVersion: augmentations/v1beta1

kind: ReplicaSet

metadata:

name: hub js-rs

spec:

imitations: 3

selector:

matchLabels:

name: hub js-configmap-rs

format:

metadata:

marks:

name: hub js-configmap-rs

spec:

containers:

- name: configmap-case

picture: jonbaier/hub express-info:latest

ports:

- containerPort: 80

name: web

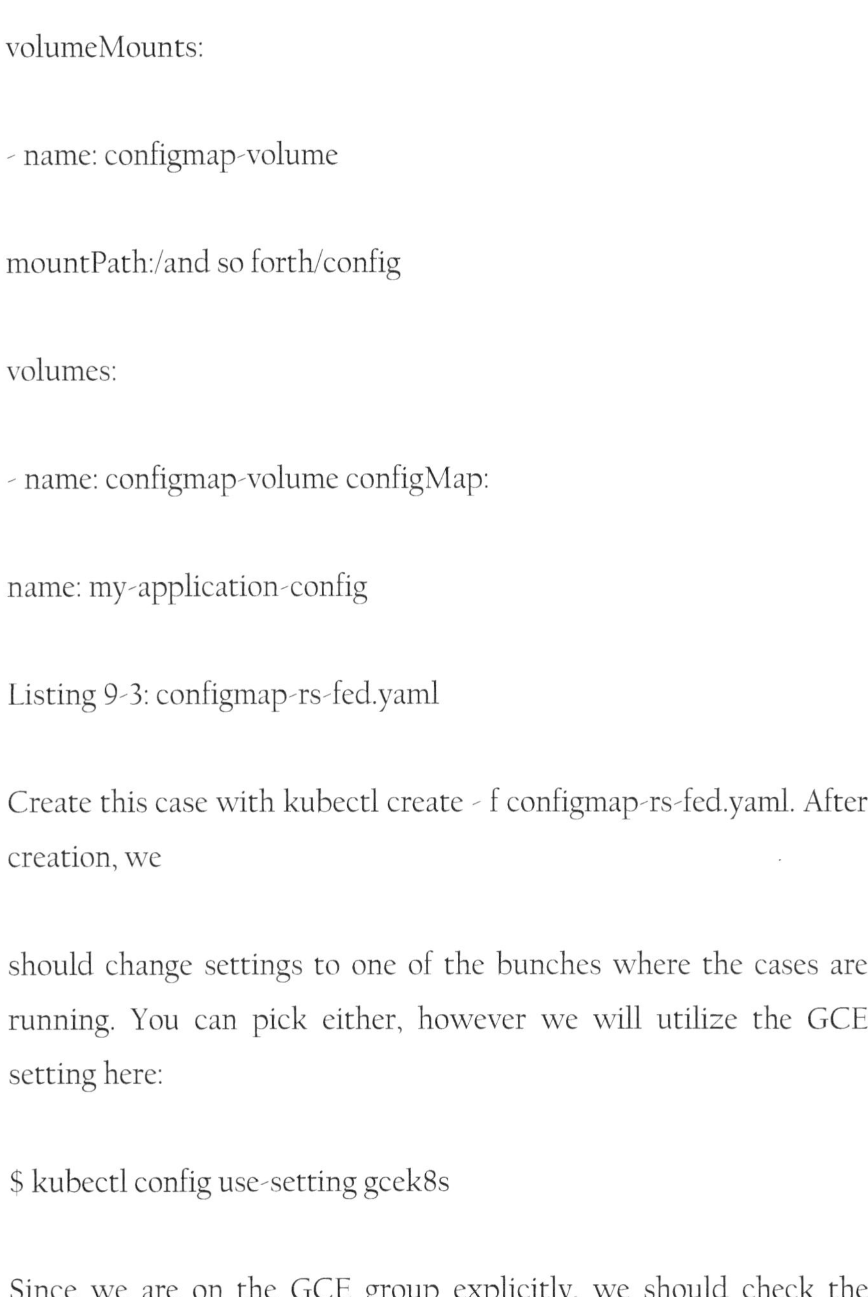

volumeMounts:

- name: configmap-volume

mountPath:/and so forth/config

volumes:

- name: configmap-volume configMap:

name: my-application-config

Listing 9-3: configmap-rs-fed.yaml

Create this case with kubectl create - f configmap-rs-fed.yaml. After creation, we

should change settings to one of the bunches where the cases are running. You can pick either, however we will utilize the GCE setting here:

$ kubectl config use-setting gcek8s

Since we are on the GCE group explicitly, we should check the configmaps here:

$ kubectl get configmaps

As should be obvious, the ConfigMap is spread locally to each bunch. Next, how about we find a case from our combined ReplicaSet:

$ kubectl get cases

How about we take one of the hub js-rs case names from the listing and run a slam shell with kubectl executive:

$ kubectl executive - it hub js-rs-6g7nj slam

At that point change registries to the/and so forth/config organizer that we set up in the case definition. Listing this index uncovers a single file with the name of the ConfigMap we defined before:

$cd/and so on/config

$ls

In the event that we, at that point show the substance of the files with the following command, we should see the worth we entered before: my-backend-administration:

$ reverberation $(cat backend-service.url)

If we somehow happened to glance in any of the units over our combined group we would see similar qualities. This is an extraordinary method to decouple arrangement from an application and appropriate it over our armada of bunches.

Other unified assets

So far we saw unified Deployments, ReplicaSets, Events, and ConfigMaps in

activity. DaemonSets, Ingress, Namespaces, Secrets, and Services are additionally upheld. Your particular arrangement will fluctuate and you may have a lot of bunches that vary from our model here. As referenced before, these assets are still in beta, so it merits spending some an opportunity to explore different avenues regarding the different asset types and understand how well the league develops are upheld for your specific blend of infrastructure.

Genuine multi-cloud

This is an exciting space to watch. As it develops it gives us a great beginning to doing multi-cloud usage and providing excess crosswise over districts, server farms, and even cloud suppliers.

While Kubernetes provides a simple and exciting way to multi-cloud infrastructure, note that generation multi-cloud requires significantly more than dispersed organizations. A full arrangement of abilities from logging and monitoring to consistence and host-hardening, there is a lot to oversee in a multi-supplier arrangement.

Genuine multi-cloud selection will require a well-arranged design, and Kubernetes steps forward in pursuing this objective.

Summary

In this section, we took a gander at the new league abilities in Kubernetes. We perceived how we can send groups to various cloud suppliers and oversee them from a single control plane. We additionally conveyed an application crosswise over groups in both AWS and GCE. While these highlights are new and still mainly in alpha and beta, we should now have the right stuff to use them as they advance and become some portion of the standard Kubernetes operating model.

In the following part, we will investigate another propelled point, security. We will cover the nuts and bolts for secure containers and likewise how to verify your Kubernetes group. We will likewise take a gander at the Secrets build, which gives us the capacity to store touchy setup information like our preceding ConfigMap model.

Chapter 10. Kubernetes Ingress

We will start with a simple scenario: You are deploying an application on Kubernetes for a company that has an online store selling products. Your application would be available at say my-online-store.com.

You build the application into a docker image and deploy it on the Kubernetes cluster as a pod in a deployment. Your application needs a database, so you deploy a MySQL database as a pod and create a service of type clusterIP called MySQL-service to make it accessible to our application. Your application is now working.

To make the application accessible to the outside world, you create another service this time of type NodePort and make your application available on a high port on the nodes in the cluster. In this example, a port 38080 is allocated for the service; the users can now access your application using the URL http://<node-ip>:38080. That setup works, and users can access the application.

Whenever traffic increases, we increase the number of replicas of the pod to handle the additional traffic, and the service takes care of splitting traffic between the pods. However, if you have deployed a production-grade application before, you should know that there are many more things involved in addition to merely splitting the traffic between the pods.

For example, we do not want the users to have to type in the IP address every time, so you configure your DNS server to point to the IP of the nodes. Your users can now access your application using the URL my-online-store.com and port 38080.

You don't want your users to have to remember port number either; however, service NodePorts can only allocate high numbered ports which are greater than 30,000. You then bring in an additional layer between the DNS server and your cluster, like a proxy server that proxies requests on port 80 to port 38080 on your nodes.

You then point your DNS to this server, and users can now access your application by simply visiting my-online-store.com.

This is if your application is hosted on Prem in your data center. Let's take a step back and see what you could do if you were in a public cloud environment like Google cloud platform. In that case, instead of creating a service of type NodeNort for your wear application, you could set it to type LoadBalancer.

When you do that, Kubernetes would still do everything that it has to do for a NodePort, which is to provision a high port for the service. In addition to that, Kubernetes also sends a request to Google cloud platform to provision a network load balancer for this service.

On receiving the request, GCP would then automatically deploy a load balancer configured to route traffic to the service ports on all nodes and return its information to Kubernetes.

The load balancer has an external IP that can be provided to users to access the application. In this case, we set the DNS to point to this IP, and users access the application using the URL my-online-store.com

Your company's business grows, and you now have new services for your customers, for example, a video streaming service. You want your users to be able to access your new video streaming service by going to my-online-store.com/watch, and you'd like to make your old application accessible at my-online-store.com/wear.

Your developers develop the new video streaming application as a completely different application as it has nothing to do with the existing one, however, to share the cluster's resources, you deploy the new application as a separate deployment within the same cluster.

You create a service called video-service of type LoadBalancer — Kubernetes provisions 38282 for this service and also provisions in network load balancer on the cloud. The new load balancer has a new IP. Remember, you must pay for each of these load balancers and having many such load balancers can inversely affect your cloud bill.

So how do you direct traffic between each of these load balancers based on the URL that the user types in?

You need yet another proxy or load balancer that can redirect traffic based on URLs to the different services. Every time you introduce a new service, you have to reconfigure the load balancer. Finally, you also need to enable SSL for your applications so your users can access your application using https.

Where do you configure that?

It can be done at different levels either at the application level itself, at the load balancer level, or the proxy server level. You don't want your developers to implement it in their applications, as they would do it in different ways. It's also an additional burden for them to develop additional codes to handle that; you want it to be configured in one place with minimal maintenance.

These configurations become challenging to manage when your application scales.

It requires involving different individuals in different teams; you need to configure your firewall rules for each new service, and it's expensive as well as for each service in a new cloud-native load balancer needs to be provisioned.

Wouldn't it be nice if you could manage all of that within the Kubernetes cluster and have that entire configuration as just another Kubernetes definition file that lives along with the rest of your application deployment files?

That's where INGRESS comes in.

Think of ingress as a layer 7 load balancer built into the Kubernetes cluster that can be configured using native Kubernetes primitives just like any other object that we've been working within Kubernetes.

Remember, even with ingress; you still need to expose it to make it accessible outside the cluster. So you still have to either publish it as a node port or with a cloud-native load balancer, but that is just a one-time configuration. Going forward, you're going to perform all your load balancing, authentication, SSL, and URL based routing configurations on the ingress controller.

So how does it work? What is it? Where is it? How can you see it, and how can you configure it? How does it load balance? How does it implement SSL?

But first, without ingress, how would you do all of these?

I will use a reverse proxy or a load balancing solution like Nginx or haproxy. I would deploy them on my Kubernetes cluster and configure them to route traffic to other services. The configuration involves defining URL routes, configuring SSL certificates, etc.

Kubernetes implement ingress in kind of the same way.

First, deploy a supported solution which happens to be any of these: Nginx, HAPROXY or trafik and then specify a set of rules to configure ingress. The solution you deploy is called as an ingress controller, and the set of rules you configure are called as ingress resources.

Ingress resources are created using definition files like the ones used to create pods deployments and services. Remember, a Kubernetes cluster does not come with an ingress controller by default, so if you create ingress resources and expect them to work, they won't.

INGRESS CONTROLLER

You do not have an ingress controller in Kubernetes by default, so you must deploy one.

What do you deploy?

There are several solutions available for ingress a few of them being GCE (which is Google's layer 7 HTTP load balancer), Nginx, contour, HAPROXY, trafik, and Istio.

Out of these, GCE and nginx are currently being supported and maintained by the Kubernetes project. In this book, we will use Nginx as an example. These ingress controllers are not just another load balancer or Nginx server; the load balancer components are just a part of it. Ingress controllers have additional intelligence built into them to monitor the Kubernetes cluster for new definitions or inverse resources and configure the Nginx server accordingly.

An Nginx controller is deployed as just another deployment in Kubernetes.

- We start with a deployment definition file named Nginx-ingress-controller with one replica and a simple pod definition template.

We will label it nginx-ingress, and the image used is nginx-ingress-controller with the right version. This is a unique build of Nginx built specifically to be used as an ingress controller in Kubernetes, so it has its own set of requirements.

Within the image, the Nginx program is stored at location /nginx-ingress-controller so you must pass that as the command to start the Nginx controller service.

If you have worked with Nginx before, you know that it has a set of configuration options such as the path to store the logs, the keepalive threshold, SSL settings, session timeout, etc. To decouple these configuration data from the Nginx controller image, you must create a config map object and pass that in.

Remember, the config map object needs not to have any entries at this point - a blank object will do, but creating one makes it easy for you to modify a configuration setting in the future. You will have to add it to this config map and not have to worry about modifying the Nginx configuration files. You must also pass into environment variables that carry the pods' name and namespace it is deployed to.

The Nginx service requires these to read the configuration data from within the pod and finally specify the ports used by the ingress controller, which happens to be 80 and 443.

We then need a service to expose the ingress controller to the external world, so we create a service of type NodePort with the Nginx ingress label selector to link the service to the deployment.

As mentioned before, the ingress controllers have additional intelligence built into them to monitor the Kubernetes cluster for ingress resources and configure the underlying Nginx server when something has changed. Still, for the ingress controller to do this, it requires a service account with the right set of permissions. For that, we create a service account with the correct roles and RoleBindings.

To summarize, with a deployment of the Nginx ingress image, a service to expose it, a config map to feed nginx data, and a service account with the right permissions to access all of these objects, we should be ready with an ingress controller in its simplest form.

INGRESS RESOURCE

Ingress resource is a set of rules and configurations applied on the ingress controller. You can configure rules to say: simply forward all incoming traffic to a single application or route traffic to different applications based on the URL. So if the user goes to my-online-store.com/wear, then route to one app or if the user visits the watch URL, then route the user to the video app, etc.

You could route users based on the domain name itself; for example, if the user visits wear.my-online-store.com, then route the user to the wear app or else route the user to the video app.

Let us look at how to configure these in a bit more detail.

The ingress resource is created with a Kubernetes definition file; in this case ingress-wear.yaml

As with any other object, we have API version, kind, metadata and spec. The API version is extensions/v1beta1.

Kind is ingress, and we will name it ingress-wear, and under spec, we have back-end.

Remember that the API version for ingress is extension/v1beta1, but this is expected to change with newer releases of Kubernetes. So when you are deploying ingress, always remember to refer to the Kubernetes documentation to know exactly the right API version for that release of Kubernetes.

So the traffic is routed to the application services and not pods directly. The backend section defines where the traffic will be routed to, so if it's a single back-end, then you don't have any rules. You can specify the service name and port of the backend wear-service.

- Create the ingress resource by running the kubectl create command.

- View the created ingress by running the kubectl get ingress command.

The new ingress is now created and routes all incoming traffic directly to the wear-service.

You use rules when you want to route traffic based on different conditions; for example, you create one rule for traffic originating from each domain or hostname. That means when users reach your cluster using the domain name my-online-store.com you can handle that traffic using rule 1.

When users reach your cluster using domain name wear.my-online-store.com you can handle that traffic using a separate rule: rule 2. Use rule 3 to handle traffic from watch.my-online-store.com and say use the fourth rule to handle everything else.

And just in case you didn't know, you could get different domain names to reach your cluster by adding multiple DNS entries, all pointing to the same ingress controller service on your Kubernetes cluster.

Within each rule you can handle different paths; for example, within rule 1, you can handle the wear path to route that traffic to the clothes application. A watch path to route traffic to the video streaming application and a third path that routes anything other than the first two to a 404 not found page.

Similarly, the second rule handles all traffic from wear.my-online-store.com. You can have path definition within this rule to route traffic based on different paths. For example, say you have different applications and services within the apparel section for shopping, returns or support.

When a user goes to wear.my-online-store.com, by default, they reach the shopping page but if they go to exchange or support URL, they reach a different back-end service.

The same goes for rule 3, where you route traffic from watch.my-online-store.com to the video streaming application, but you can have additional paths in it such as movies or TV.

Finally, anything other than the ones listed here will go to the 4th rule that would show a 404 not found error page. Remember we have rules at the top for each host or domain name, and within each rule, you have different paths to route traffic based on the URL.

How to Configure Ingress Resources in Kubernetes

- We start with a similar definition file, this time under spec, we start with a set of rules. Our requirement here is to handle all traffic coming into my-online-store.com and route them based on the URL path, so we need a single URL for this since we are only handling traffic to a single domain name, which is my-online-store.com. In this case, under rules, we have one item which is an http rule in which we specify different paths.

- Paths is an array of multiple items; one path for each URL, then we move the back-end we used in the first example under the first path. The backend specification remains the same; it has a service name and service port. Similarly, we create a similar back-end entry to the second URL path for the watch service to route all traffic coming in through the watch URL to the watch service.

- Create the ingress resource using the kubectl create command.

- Once created, view additional details about the ingress resource by running the kubectl describe ingress command.

You now see two back-end URLs under the rules and the backend service they are pointing to just as we created it. If you look closely at the output of this command, you see that there is something about a default back-end. What might that be?

If a user tries to access a URL that does not match any of these rules, then the user is directed to the service specified as the default backend. In this case, it happens to be a service named default-http-backend, so you must remember to deploy such a service.

Back in your application, say a user visits the URL my-online-store.com/listen or eat, and you don't have audio streaming or a food delivery service; you might want to show them a nice message. You can do this by configuring a default backend service to display a 404 not found error page in addition to any message you might have for the user.

The third type of configuration is using domain names or hostnames. We start by creating a similar definition file for ingress. Now that we have two domain names, we create two rules one for each domain. To split traffic by domain name, we use the host field. The host field in each rule matches the specified value with the domain name used in the request URL and routes traffic to the appropriate back-end. In this case, note that we only have a single back-end path for each rule.

All traffic from these domain names will be routed to the appropriate back-end irrespective of the URL path used. You can still have multiple path specifications in each of these to handle different URL paths.

Chapter 11. Continuous Integration And Continuous Delivery

Kubernetes Continuous Integration / Continuous Delivery (CI/CD) pipeline.

I combine Ansible, Terraform, and Kubernetes on AWS to run production Microservices. In this chapter, I will share GitOps workflows and automation with Terraform Kubernetes CI/CD pipeline. The main point in this section is managing a staging and production CI/CD environment with Terraform.

It's all about handling the execution engines (Docker Swarm, Kubernetes, etc.) that checkout source code and executes in containers and the launcher that executes and monitors commands inside the container with Terraform.

The target is a GitOps based Infrastructure as a Code (IaC) that handles 52,000 plus builds per day, and 26,000 plus daily git commits as a single shared entry point, supporting multiple languages and handles both virtual machine and container-based builds and deployment.

Building containers and deploying to your clusters is tedious; deploying docker images staging environment is even harder.

Uninterrupted Delivery

Continuous Delivery will enable software development teams to move faster and adapt to users' needs faster by reducing the inherent friction associated with releasing software changes.

When it comes to the software development business, there is no such thing as a 'final product' simply because the search for new features and functions by both the end-user and customer is ongoing. There is constant evolution as new solutions are found for fixing errors in production code, fixing bugs, and software configuration management.

To offer the user optimal results with overheads kept to a minimum continuous delivery and DevOps should complement one another. Jenkins gives developers the option to make changes to the source code according to the needs of the user.

The source code is located in a shared repository. Jenkins centralize operations and engineering and is, without a doubt, one of the most powerful tools being used for this purpose by software developers. When compared to tools like BuildBot and Travis, for example, the goal of continuous delivery is much simpler to obtain with Jenkins.

Adopting continuous delivery allows DevOps teams to move many orders of magnitude faster, reducing outages, improving software quality and security. Applications are infrastructure aware (aka "cloud-native"), auto-scale seamlessly with the peaks and troughs of customer demand, self-heal when things go wrong and deliver a great experience to customers — no matter where they are in the world.

Using Terraform commands, remote state backends, and version control, a declarative coding style is used to manage infrastructure, declaring cluster state in YAML files that fit with existing workflows.

On the staging environment, a developer can — with one or two invocations of CLI scripts — easily deploy that build to the production environment. The software project pipelines are created by a Terraform module.

It is streamlined to build system designed to enable Continuous Delivery to production at scale for dynamic infrastructure.

In my experience working Terraform Kubernetes CI/CD pipeline deployment pipelines that continuously test, integrate, and deploy code to production greatly reduce the risk of errors and reduce the time to get feedback to developers. The challenge confronting many groups had been that pipelines were bulky to set up and maintained. The process is based on the idea of a release-candidate progressing through a series of gates.

Automating a Continuous Integration / Continuous Delivery pipeline has the following advantages:

- At each stage, the confidence in the release candidate is enhanced.
- Making deployment pipelines easy
- Optimizing for trunk development
- Making rolling back easy
- The mechanism to store structured build data for later use (last deployed version, test coverage, etc.)
- Built-in metric collecting
- System-wide templates to enable getting started quickly

- Log analysis to provide insights to developers

Integration with a continuous deployment pipeline

Kubernetes offers a sophisticated platform for making cloud deployments easy. Low-stress deployments are actually the cornerstone of Continuous Delivery practices. Engineering teams are able to iterate quickly, experiment, and keep the customers happy all at the same time having the means to rollback, deploy, and orchestrate software releases safely and reliably.

The continuous delivery of service-oriented software systems is made possible by a number of industry-standard deployment strategies. Under this topic, we will describe a number of existing techniques and strategies and discuss their pros, cons, and caveats. For each of the strategies, we will also give an example that can be implemented and verified using Codefresh Kubernetes integration features.

List of strategies:

- Recreate

- Ramped Deployments

- Blue/Green Deployments

- Canary Releases

- A/B Testing

Setting the Terms Straight

Before we start, it's important to agree on the terminology.

Kubernetes has a controller object called Deployment. Its primary purpose is to give declarative desired state management for underlying Pods and Replica Sets.

Basically, a Deployment defines:

- The Pod required to execute (i.e., containers, ports, and system resources)

- The number of instances the Pod should have

- All the metadata related to underlying objects

The Deployment object also has a property named 'Strategy' which can be of 2 types: either 'Recreate' or 'Rolling Update.'

In this section, the term deployment strategy does not mean the mentioned K8S object property.

While the usage of K8S technical concepts will be showcased, the intentions to describe what the general continuous application deployment strategies are and explain how they can be put into effect on top of the Kubernetes platform.

Recreate

Fair enough, this is not a real continuous deployment strategy. It's more like the old-fashioned installation or upgrade process. You can stop all active and running application instances and then spin up the instances with the new version.

(In Kubernetes this is implemented by deployment. Spec. strategy. Type of the same name-Recreate whereas all existing Pods are killed before new ones are created.)

The downside:

This deployment approach permits downtime to occurs, while the old versions are getting shut down and the new versions are just starting up.

The upside:

The upside of this approach is the cleanliness and conceptual simplicity. At no time should we have to manage more than one application version in parallel? No API versioning issues, there's no data scheme incompatibilities to think about.

Applicability:

This strategy is most suitable for non-critical systems where downtime is acceptable and comes at no high cost. Our development environment is an example of this. It's pertinent to remember, though that if we architect our services for continuous deployment, we should be testing their upgrade and failover behaviors as early as possible. Which means that we are better off using the same rollout procedure for all environment maturity levels.

Ramped Deployment:

This is simply another term for the rolling update. An important thing worthy to note is that this is only applicable when your service is horizontally scaled, i.e., running in more than one instance. If this is really the case, then instances running the old version get retired as new instances with the new version get spun up.

This should, of course, be followed by at least some kind of a basic health check in order to verify that the new instances are ready to provide services.

In Kubernetes, health checks can be defined as a readiness-Probe.

Once an instance is considered ready to serve - the traffic will be sent to it.

If the new instances are not found to be healthy — this strategy provides a smooth rollback procedure: old version instances get scaled back to their original capacity as new versions get killed off.

It is important to note that the old and the new version of our code run parallel in te rollout process. Full backward-compatibility of our API and schema changes or careful API versioning whenever backward compatibility gets broken is therefore required.

The downside:

Version simultaneousness concerns: -Backward compatibility and API versioning aren't easy to implement and require careful testing.

System comprehensibility: - Issues arising during the transition process will be significantly harder to debug and recreate.

Resource cost: - If we don't want any impact on the quality of service, we'll need to bring up the new instances while the old ones are still running.

This automatically implies that there will be a resource usage peak during the rollout process. Dealing with these peaks has become much easier in the age of cloud infrastructure, but still — resources don't come for free.

The upside:

Smooth and Slow application code rollout across all servers with integrated health checks and no downtime involved.

In-place rollback should be available in case the deployment is unsuccessful.

Applicability:

As already stated, ramped deployments only make sense when the deployed application is horizontally scaled.

Additionally, ramped deployments are fantastic when the new versions are backward compatible, both API and data-wise. And when your system is truly service-oriented, with clear context boundaries, API versioning, and eventual consistency support built-in.

Blue/Green (aka Red/Black) Deployment

In this method, we always manage two versions of our production environment. One of them is considered 'blue,' i.e., this is the version that is now live. The new versions are usually deployed to the 'green' replica of the environment.

After we run all the necessary tests and verifications to make sure the 'blue' environment is ready we just flip over the traffic, so 'green' becomes 'blue,' and 'blue' becomes 'green.'

Note: This strategy introduces a new concern we didn't mention earlier, which is "managing multiple deployment environments." While standard practice in CI/CD, this adds another level of complexity to our deployment pipeline.

The downside:

Resource duplication: In this technique, we're maintaining at least two full versions of our environment at all times.

Management overhead: This strategy can become very resource-intensive and heavy to manage if each environment encompasses multiple service components.

We can, of course, create an environment for each service, but then the matrix of interrelated environments becomes quite hard to comprehend.

Data synchronization between the two environments is challenging. Especially while the 'green' environment is still under test.

The upside:

This has a very low-stress deployment since we never deploy to production.

No downtime because traffic redirection occurs on the fly.

Availability of extensive production-like testing prior to switching over.

Seamless rolling-back process in case something goes wrong is as easy as just flipping the traffic switch back to the 'blue' environment. Data sync taken into account of course.

Applicability

When working with a fully autonomous service or within a system without too many services, this can be a good choice.

The first reason being that two copies of a full application environment can be held. (In K8s each of these can be managed as a separate namespace.)

Secondly, a pair of environments for each service can be maintained, the service can be testes in isolation, and the traffic switch can be flipped when the new version is verified.

Canary Releases

Canary releases received their name from coal miners' practice of carrying a canary in a cage down the mine. If there were poisonous gases in the mine- they would kill the canary before killing the humans. Similarly, a canary release will allow us to test for potential problems before impacting our entire production system or user base.

Procedures:

We deploy new version into the same environment as the production system.

We then re-route a small part of production traffic to be served by the new instance. (This is also known as 'testing in production.') The routing can be absolutely percentage-based or driven by specific crit factors such as user location, type of client, and billing properties. This kind of deployment needs careful application performance monitoring and error rate measurements. The collected metrics actually define the so-called canary quality threshold.

If the application is behaving as expected, meaning the threshold is passed, we can transfer even more traffic to the new version by spinning up gradually. Additional canary quality gateways can still be introduced along the way.

The downside:

The variation of blue-green with fine-tuned traffic splitting and more meticulous quality threshold enforcement is the canary. Therefore, all the complexities of blue-green are present and amplified.

It needs heightened system observability, which is desirable but entails substantial effort to achieve.

The upside:

Observability: This is a must for canary strategy. Once you build up the needed infrastructure, your ability to experiment, test hypotheses, and identify issues will provide a lot of power.

Ability to test actual production traffic: Creating production-like testing environments is hard. With Canary, there's definitely no need to do the same.

It has the ability to release a version to a subset of users.

Fail fast: Canary allows us to deploy straight into production and fail fast if something goes wrong. Yes, care should be taken, so the new app version does not cause data corruption.

Applicability:

The usage of this is recommended if you've already invested in modern monitoring and logging tools. Maybe less applicable if your deployments involve schema changes as you don't want to change production schemas just to test a new version.

A/B Testing

Frankly speaking, this isn't really a deployment strategy. More of the market research approach enabled by a deployment technology very similar to what we described as Canary.

We deploy a new version alongside the old one and use traffic splitting techniques to route some of the client requests to the new version.

We thereafter compare the business, application, or system performance metrics between the two versions in order to understand what works best.

A/B testing enables us to not only compare old Vs. New but also permits to deploy multiple versions of the new feature and analyze which one yields better business results.

The downside:

Heightened system complexity that is very difficult to debug and analyze.

It involves advanced load-balancing and traffic splitting techniques.

The upside:

It allows for intelligent market and customer behavior analysis.

Several application versions can also be deployed in parallel.

Applicability:

Use this when you have already achieved continuous delivery of features as it is best used with continuous deployments approach like feature toggling, which are application based. It requires agile Ops teams to swiftly produce autonomous features that can be easily rolled back or forward. And of course, virtually everything that I previously said about observability also applies here too.

Conclusion

Kubernetes is scalable containerized workloads onto a platform. While Kubernetes' structure and set of elements can appear daunting, feature set, versatility, and their ability are unparalleled in the world that is open-minded.

You can start to design systems that leverage the capabilities of this system by knowing the building blocks fit together.

The container applications Kubernetes is among the top-rated projects of times, and its adoption has grown in the past couple of decades. After working in an organization that's been growing and building applications with Kubernetes because 2015, it is observed that engineers go through all stages of this Kubernetes adoption cycle, from unbroken excitement about the possibilities, this technology provides to sleepless nights solving issues with all our clusters and deployments.

If Kubernetes is your right, there's no easy answer option for you. It is dependent upon your requirements and priorities, and lots of reasons weren't even mentioned here.

If you're beginning with a new job, if you operate in a startup which plans to scale and wishes to grow more than only a fast mvp or should you have to update a legacy program, Kubernetes may be a fantastic choice providing you a great deal of flexibility, power, and scalability.

Since abilities need to be obtained but, it requires an investment of time, and workflows must get established on your dev team.

If done correctly, nevertheless, investing the time will pay off later on higher productivity, due to support quality level and a more motivated workforce.

Whatever the situation, you must make an educated choice, and there are numerous excellent reasons. I hope this article can assist you in becoming closer to making you the proper choice.

However, there are some downsides of Kubernetes with it that are discussed here:

Kubernetes could be overkill for simple software

Kubernetes is to run applications in a cloud surrounding on a scale.

But if you don't intend to come up with anything complicated for a big or spread crowd (therefore, you aren't building a global online store with thousands of clients as an instance) or using higher computing resource demands (e. G. , machine learning software), there's very little advantage for you from your technical capacity of k8s.

Let us say you wish to come up with a site revealing place and the opening hours of your enterprise. Then Kubernetes should not be used by you since this isn't what it was created for.

An individual cannot say that each machine learning application should operate with Kubernetes without a website needs to. It's simply probable it will be valuable in the first case than in another person.

Kubernetes is very intricate and will decrease productivity

CPSIA information can be obtained
at www.ICGtesting.com
Printed in the USA
BVHW040452010521
606222BV00001B/200